PANCHAYATI RAJ IN JAMMU AND KASHMIR

PANCHAYATI RAJ
IN
JAMMU AND KASHMIR

Edited by

George Mathew

Foreword by

Farooq Abdullah

Institute of Social Sciences

and

CONCEPT PUBLISHING COMPANY, NEW DELHI-110059

First Published 1990

Published by
Ashok Kumar Mittal
Concept Publishing Company
A/15-16, Commercial Block, Mohan Garden
New Delhi-110 059

Layout by
Institute of Social Sciences
B-7/18 Safdarjung Enclave
New Delhi-110 029

Printed at
Taj Press
Delhi

Dedicated

to

The People

of

Jammu and Kashmir

Foreword

THE State of Jammu and Kashmir has the distinction of bringing about the first ever agrarian revolution in India by adopting the measure of 'land to tiller'. This step fulfilled the major pledge made by the people's manifesto of National Conference enshrined in 'Naya Kashmir'. This revolutionary stride would have yielded tremendous results in ameliorating the conditions of rural poor, had it been coupled with the efforts of strengthening the process of democratic decentralisation through the panchayati raj institutions in the State of Jammu and Kashmir. History bears testimony to the fact as to why it was not to be so.

The Jammu and Kashmir Panchayati Raj Act, 1989 is yet another endeavour to revive the efforts to take the democratic process to the grassroots level. It is an attempt to complete the process of transforming the rural scene which was started by National Conference some forty years ago. Our Government, initiated a process of equitable development of far flung areas in various districts of the State. The Panchayati Raj Act, 1989 aims at initiating a process where the development plans will emanate from below rather than trickle down from above. We shall strive to ensure the political participation of masses at the lowest rungs of society and realize the dream of endowing economic benefits to all in an equitable manner. The role of Panchayats in this herculean task cannot be underestimated and needs to be realized in full measure.

The culmination of the discussions on Jammu and Kashmir Panchayati Raj Bill, which has now become an Act, has resulted in the compilation of this book. It contains valuable contributions by luminaries and provides great insights into philosophical foundations of the goals and working of Panchayati Raj in the country as well as analysis of the reasons for failure of this great social system.

I am deeply grieved that Shri S.K. Dey is no more with us. I still recall his emotion choked, sincere and illuminating speech at the inaugural session of the Panchayati Raj Seminar in Srinagar organised by the Institute of Social Sciences to launch this study. His long association with Kashmir and love for Kashmiris have left lasting impressions on us. The builder of modern India, Pandit Jawaharlal Nehru relied on this visionary to build democracy from Gram Sabha to Lok Sabha. Our tribute to this great wizard of panchayati raj would be to implement the Act in Jammu and Kashmir in right earnest for establishing institutions of local self government which will give power to the people.

It is my cherished desire to see the youth in our rural areas actively involved in the development and affairs of the State. I have faith in their capacity to improve the quality of life of our people. The vibrant local self governments will provide opportunities to fulfil their urges and aspirations. Participatory democracy is *sine qua non* of improving the quality of life of our people.

I want to mention here that in pursuance of this objective we propose to change the constitution of the District Planning Boards. These Planning Boards will have elected chairmen rather than nominated, as in the present Act.

Our experience of panchayati raj bring two important facts to the fore. First, the administrators as well as the politicians must be oriented to a new culture of decentralisation of power. They have to bring about a radical change in their attitude to make this new experiment a success. Secondly, as Shri Nirmal Mukarji aptly points out, means and methods are to be devised to federalize the national planning process. These two requirements are essential for the survival and development of panchayati raj as the cornerstone of India's federalism.

I am grateful to Dr George Mathew for initiating a debate on the Jammu and Kashmir Panchayati Raj Bill. In fact, it was through his persuasion and the dedicated efforts of his colleagues in the Institute of Social Sciences, New Delhi that we could draw upon the expertise and wisdom of a large group from Jammu and Kashmir and the rest of the country.

I congratulate the Institute of Social Sciences, New Delhi for bringing out this publication which will serve as an important source book on Panchayati Raj in Jammu and Kashmir in the context of the emerging trend at the national level.

Jammu — DR. FAROOQ ABDULLAH

December, 1989.

The Contributors

S. K. Dey: Union Minister for Community Development, Panchayati Raj and Co-operation (1956-1966), and later special Adviser to the United Nations on Rural Development.

Nirmal K. Mukarji: Governor of Punjab and Union Territory of Chandigarh. Formerly Cabinet Secretary, Government of India; Chief Secretary, Government of Jammu and Kashmir.

Mohammad Shafi: Minister for Agriculture and Rural Development, Government of Jammu and Kashmir.

Riyaz Punjabi: Professor and Chairman, Department of Distance Education, Dean, Faculty of Non-formal Education, University of Kashmir, Srinagar.

Balraj Puri: Author, Commentator, Social activist. Director, Institute of Jammu and Kashmir Affairs, Jammu.

Sushma Choudhary: Secretary-cum-Commissioner, Ministry of Agriculture and Rural Development, Government of Jammu and Kashmir.

Alice Jacob: Director, Indian Law Institute, New Delhi.

M C Mehta: Advocate, Supreme Court of India.

Abhijit Datta: Professor, Urban Administration and Development and Municipal Finance, Indian Institute of Public Administration, New Delhi.

Mohammad Sultan: Assistant Professor, Department of Economics, University of Kashmir, Srinagar.

Sreemay Basu: Visiting Professor and Head, Centre for Analysis and Systems Studies, School of Planning and Architecture, New Delhi.

Arun Ghosh: Member, Planning Commission. Former Vice-Chairman, State Planning Board, Government of West Bengal.

CONTENTS

Introduction

The earth whose dust conceals the fire of the chinar in its conscience
Can never go cold, nor ever lose its self respect

—Iqbal

"FOR the outside world Kashmir's image is that of a tension ridden, problem State. Very little is known about the positive developments in the State like the steps taken to ensure grass roots level democracy", said I.K. Gujral, participating in the seminar organised in Srinagar by the Institute of Social Sciences in October 1988 to discuss the Panchayati Raj Bill introduced in the Jammu and Kashmir Assembly on April 2, 1988. The seminar, held at the Sher-i-Kashmir International Conference Hall and attended by a group of experts and others concerned with the evolution and development of grass roots level democracy in the country had the following aims:

1. understanding of the Panchayati Raj Bill of 1988 in the specific historical and social setting of Jammu and Kashmir.
2. assessment of the emerging trends in the Indian federal structure *vis*-a-*vis*, local self-government systems.
3. study of the strength and weakness of specific aspects of the Bill like (a) Panchayat Adalat, (b) Panchayati Raj Finances and (c) District Planning.
4. evaluation of the Jammu and Kashmir model in the context of experiences in the matter of other States like West Bengal and Karnataka.

It goes to the credit of the Chief Minister Dr. Farooq Abdullah and the National Conference leadership, especially Mr Mohammad Shafi, Minister for Agriculture and Rural Development that before the Bill was passed in March 1989 by the Assembly (the Governor gave his assent in July 1989), they invited discussion on its provisions by persons concerned with grass roots level democracy and the Indian federal structure. The Chief Minister, his colleagues in the cabinet and the party and the select committee took serious note of the suggestions made at various levels and incorporated them in the Act of 1989. This book is the outcome of the free but critical exchange of views on the subject between the political leadership in Jammu and Kashmir and the intellectuals within the State and the rest of the country.

Prior to the Srinagar seminar, in August 1988, a consultation to elicit expert opinion on various provisions of the bill was organised by the Institute of Social Sciences at the Centre for Policy Research, New Delhi. It was attended by Nirmal Mukarji, Inder Mohan, Pai Panandekar, M. C. Mehta, Alice Jacob, Abhijit Dutta, Jawahar Sircar and the author. The Jammu and Kashmir Government was represented by Mohammad Shafi and Sushma Chaudhary, Commissioner, Agricultural Production incharge of Panchayati Raj and Rural Development. The summary of the discussions and the notes prepared by the participants was the source material for the preparation of the Srinagar meet.

The Jammu and Kashmir Legislation assumes special significance because it comes as a sequel to the efforts in several States in the past decade to take a fresh look at the working of the panchayati raj institutions as instruments of devolution of power to the people at the village level. It was thirty years ago that the first legislation on the subject in the shape of the Jammu and Kashmir Panchayat Act of 1958 was enacted. That the Government found it necessary to revise and review it in the light of experience speaks volumes for its political will and flair for dynamism. While the 1958 Act was limited in purpose to provide for a suitable administrative structure for the village panchayats in the State, the 1988 Bill envisaged significant changes at the district level and below. The thrust was on the entire gamut of the local self-government system and not development functions alone. Therefore, the goal of the new legislation was "to promote and develop panchayati raj in the State *as an instrument of vigorous local self-government* to secure the effective participation of the people in the decision-making process and for overseeing implementation of developmental programmes" (emphasis added).

This change of emphasis was in consonance with the new thinking on the subject at the national level.

The period between October 2, 1959, when Jawaharlal Nehru inaugurated Panchayati Raj in Rajasthan hailing it as "the most revolutionary and historical step in the context of our India" and his disappearance from the scene in 1964, saw the emergence of first generation Panchayati Raj in the country after independence. It followed the recommendations of the Balwant Rai Committee (1958) which led to the establishment of panchayats in different States raising the prospect of a *Grama Swaraj*. S.K. Dey, the first Minister of Panchayati Raj, was optimistic that panchayats would become a way of life with the people and will see the flowering of people's power from Grama Sabha to the Lok Sabha. After Nehru, however, the dream faded. The reason for the decline of the panchayati raj system is well known and has been the subject of analysis by many scholars.[1]

For about 13 years until 1977 Panchayati Raj was the whipping boy of all those who wanted to see it discredited. It became a veritable incarnation of evil in the village with State after State letting the organisations decay and fall by the wayside. Perhaps an exception of sorts during this period were Maharashtra and Gujarat, where the panchayats survived.

The appointment of the Asoka Mehta Committee in 1977 marked a turning point in the fortunes of the system, both conceptually and in practice. A second generation panchayats began to grow when the West Bengal Government took the initiative in 1978 to act on the recommendations of the Asoka Mehta Committee and revamp the system in the State. Karnataka followed the West Bengal example and soon Andhra Pradesh also opened a new chapter. And now the breeze has started blowing from Kashmir.

The latest in this effort to revitalise the panchayati raj system and make the local self-government meaningful is the Jammu and Kashmir Act, 1989.

The vital difference between the first generation and second generation of panchayats is the shift in emphasis from development *per se* to self-government in its full meaning. The Balwant Rai Mehta Committee made development central to the panchayat

1. For a detailed discussion see author's Introduction in *Panchayati Raj in Karnataka Today: Its National Dimensions*, Concept, New Delhi, 1986.

system, while the attempt in West Bengal, Karnataka, Andhra Pradesh and now Jammu and Kashmir is to make panchayati raj genuine political institutions and thus the crux of self-government with all its ramifications, a microcosm of the State itself.

The State Governments cannot establish full-fledged panchayati raj without adequate constitutional safeguards. In all the States where devolution of power to the village was attempted the concentration of power at the Centre proved an impediment. For instance, Abdul Nazir Sab, the Minister for Panchayati Raj in Karnataka in the Janata Government said in 1985, "Soon we realised that within the limitations imposed by the Constitution, the ideology of 'Four Pillar State'--village, district, state and centre--could not be implemented *in toto* by the State Government. . . . Without a constitutional amendment guaranteeing the 'Four Pillar State', our efforts may not be as fruitful as we desire. In my opinion this is the major question the intellectuals of this country must ponder over. They must create a public debate on the necessity of a Constitutional amendment".[2]

All those concerned with Panchayati Raj have been pleading for a specific constitutional provision for panchayati raj so that panchayati raj institutions invigorated by regular elections, periodically held, are also made financially viable.

It was against that background that the Congress(I) Government's much trumpeted 64th Constitutional Amendment Bill to confer statutory status on the Panchayati Raj was introduced in Parliament in May 1989.[3] The Bill introduced without due spade work raised the issues of federalism as a prerequisite for decentralisation of power.

The Congress(I) had two basic compulsions for introducing the ill-fated bill. First, in West Bengal, Karnataka and Andhra Pradesh, there is perceptible impact on the lives of the people of the functioning of the second generation of panchayati raj. The Congress(I) leadership at the Centre began to recognise the growing

---

2. Abdul Nazir Sab, "Towards a Four Pillar State" in *Panchayati Raj in Karnataka Today*, op.cit., pp. 50-53.

3. The Constitution (64th Amendment) Bill was introduced in the Lok Sabha on May 15, 1990. It secured two-thirds votes in the lower house but was defeated in the Rajya Sabha on October 15, 1990. Making this an issue, Congress(I) dissolved the Lok Sabha and went to polls in November 1989.

popularity of the non-Congress(I) governments in these States, besides the attention they received nationally for making devolution of power a practicality. Most of the Congress(I) State Governments, on the other hand, were the objects of censure for keeping the local bodies in hibernation either by not holding elections for decades or by superseding elected bodies and putting the grass roots level organisations in charge of civil servants. So with a view to retrieving the lost ground with the electorate, the government suddenly hit on the panchayati raj bill.

Secondly, at least a few at the helm of affairs in the Congress(I) began to realise the evils and ramifications of concentration of power. The political and social implications of centralised power were becoming transparently debilitating. The cup was nearly full. On the economic front, for instance, the former Prime Minister had to admit that of every rupee earmarked to development only 15 paise reached the target group. Without proper functioning of the local bodies the growing frustration among the people could not be stemmed.

But the Congress(I) – sponsored constitutional Amendment Bill drafted and introduced in haste sadly missed the wood for the trees. The report of the Committee[4] appointed by Shri V. P. Singh, the then leader of Opposition to examine the 64th Constitutional Amendment Bill is a seminal document on the subject. Its conclusions have an important bearing on future Indian federal polity in the context of our renewed commitment to revitalise local self-government bodies.

The following critical observations of the committee may be noted:

1. The Bill even within its limited ambit, contained a mass of details which should have been left to legislation by the States in the light of local circumstances obtaining in each State. The bill, therefore amounts to undue imposition of uniformity on the States for it contained provisions about such matters as how the constituencies should be delimited or how chairpersons of the panchayats should be elected.

---

4. The Committee consisted of S. R. Bommai (Chairman), Nirmal Mukarji, L. C. Jain, K. S. Krishnamurthy, George Mathew and B. K. Chandrasekhar. The Committee was appointed on June 13, 1989 and submitted its report on July 10, 1989

A constitutional amendment—on a subject primarily concerning the States – should have confined itself to bare essentials.

2. The Bill proceeded on the entirely unwarranted assumption that it would be possible for the States to pass down to the Panchayats a viable administrative and financial devolution package without the Centre doing anything about Centre-States relations. Meaningful decentralisation below the State level can take place only in conjunction with an equally meaningful decentralisation from the Centre to the States.
3. At the heart of the decentralisation issue is the pressing need for a new financial regime between the Centre, the States and sub-State units of self-government, whether Panchayats or local bodies in urban areas. While governments at each level must raise resources on their own to the extent of the powers available to them, the relatively strong financial position deliberately allotted to the Centre by the Constitution makes it imperative that there should be a rational scheme of financial devolution from the Centre downwards which strengthens democratic self-governance at all levels. The Constitution should guarantee that a minimum of fifty per cent of the Centre's aggregate revenue resources should devolve to the States, and similarly a minimum of fifty per cent of each State's aggregate revenue resources should devolve to Panchayats and urban local bodies.
4. There should be a rational arrangement for the sharing of resources available to governments through market borrowing. The best way to do so would be to set up a National Credit Council composed of representatives of Central and State Governments, the Reserve Bank of India and the National Planning Commission with full authority to decide how such sharing should take place.
5. There must be a new planning regime under which planning is viewed as 'national' rather than 'central' activity. The Planning Commission should pay more attention to major policy questions, including hitherto excluded matters like the right balance between defence and development. In regard to State plans, the Planning Commission should confine itself to overall dimensions and their major segments relating to infrastructure, such as power, major irrigation and communications. There must be an end to planning from above.

State plans, in particular, should be built from below, the area plans of panchayats and urban local governments forming the base.

6. Co-operatives were recognised from the beginning of the planning era as companion institutions to Panchayats, i.e., as instruments of economic democracy. The essence of a co-operative organisation is that it must be controlled democratically by its membership. The report of the Committee on Co-operative Law (1987) needs to be made public so that co-operatives can be infused with fresh life after a full national debate.
7. Two important aspects: (1) the pivotal role of the *gram sabha* comprising all eligible voters in a village and (2) *nyaya panchayats* for dispensing speedy justice to the people at the village level find no mention in the Bill. The States would be well advised to give due place to these two basic institutions in their legislations.
8. The State legislatures should ensure that elected units of self-government, panchayats or urban local bodies, are squarely in control of the administriative staff dealing with functions devolved on them.
9. If there is a case for reservation for women in the panchayats, and the committee favours reservation for them of one-third of the number of seats in a panchayat, there is an equally valid case for similar reservation for women not only in urban local governments but also in the State legislatures and Parliament.
10. The move to extend the jurisdiction of the Election Commission to panchayat elections is commendable but steps should be taken to make this constitutional authority more independent. To achieve this purpose, the Commission should have the right and duty to report to Parliament and the State legislatures about the conduct of elections at different levels. This would generate healthy debate on the problems encountered and the remedies, if any, suggested by the Commission, without the Central Government standing in the way.
11. The move to extend the jurisdiction of another constitutional authority, the Comptroller and Auditor-General of India is also commendable. In order that he too may be vested with greater independence, his reports should be submitted

> directly to Parliament and the State legislatures. Experience has shown that inconvenient reports are not promptly placed before Parliament or the State Legislature, thus offending the principle of open governance and denying to the people the corrective that might be available from a timely open debate.

The underlying issue is that any move to revitalise the local bodies and introduce a new system of governance below the State level can be effective only as part of genuine federalism in theory and practice at the national level. In the absence of it, such measures are just form without content. For the J & K measure to succeed, the Centre must show exceptional understanding on the issues touched upon by the Bommai Committee.

It is encouraging that Jammu and Kashmir provides a congenial setting for the success of measures like Panchayati Raj.

The State has seen more radical social reform than in many other states in the country. The economic backwardness of Kashmir tended to give a radical turn to its freedom movement. Although the National Conference was predominantly middle class in composition, it found its main support in the peasantry and the artisans. This drove the Kashmiri leadership to political and economic radicalism. Its programme was enshrined in the historic document called "The New Kashmir", which became the source of National Conference policies and programmes.

One of the first steps taken by the first J & K Assembly was to pass what became the most drastic piece of land reform in India. Jawaharlal Nehru had said about this reform:

> I confess that I look with some envy on the speed and clarity with which they (Kashmir Government) have performed this task there, considering the enormous trouble we have had in the various States of India, the difficulties, the obstruction and the delays that we had to face, and so, I became a little envious when I saw this was done in Kashmir.[5]

The tempo for progressive development has not slackened. A recent study by Dr. Girish Kumar of the Institute of Social Sciences

---

5. Quoted by P. N. Dhar in "Historical Realities" *Seminar* (58), June 1964, p. 14.

on the Status of Women and Children has shown that the Jammu and Kashmir has a higher female literacy rate than several north Indian States like Bihar, Rajasthan and Uttar Pradesh. Jammu and Kashmir's infant mortality rate is significantly lower than the national average. The public expenditure on health in the State is more than three times the corresponding expenditure at the national level.

Given this social development, the new Act should give a new thrust and direction to the State. The measure ensuring people's participation in the affairs of the State should pull the State out of the political turmoil in which, unfortunately, it has found itself of late. Moreover, the panchayati raj is a sure way to protect Kashmiri culture and identity.

Broadly, the book is divided into two sections, the first dealing with general issues in a national perspective and the second focusing on the State specifically.

We were fortunate to have with us at the seminar the doyen of panchayati raj in India Shri S. K. Dey. Dynamic as he always has been, his address at the inaugural session will be remembered for the sheer eloquence with which he expressed his relationship with Kashmir and the depth in which he analysed his personal involvement in the panchayati raj system from the beginning in the Nehru days. The transcript of his brilliant speech forms the first chapter of the book. It was the last public speech of such a magnificent public figure in the cause of panchayati raj, the cause which he cherished all along. He had been a guide and philosopher of the Institute in our pursuit of studying panchayati raj.

Minister Mohammad Shafi's contribution: 'Revival of Democratic Tradition' is his keynote address at the seminar. He raises several vital questions regarding the implementation of the reform and reiterates rightly that the ultimate success of decentralisation depends upon the political leadership and its sustained commitment to the principle.

Nirmal Mukarji argues for a district government system below the State level in the changed socio-political situation. He feels that unless we 'wind up the colonial dispensation of district officer' rule, there will be no revolution in the system of governance. The chapter on political parties in panchayati raj by this writer pleads for party-based participation in the elections below the State level.

The rest of the chapters are a critique of the bill dealing with specific aspects of its provisions, history and cultural context of the

State and the local administration. Balraj Puri, Mohammad Sultan, Alice Jacob, M. C. Mehta, Riyaz Punjabi, Abhijit Dutta, Sushma Chaudhary and Sreemay Basu who are specialists in the respective areas have ably dealt with them. Finally, Arun Ghosh takes the reader to the rich experience of West Bengal in the planning process at district level which has a few important lessons for Jammu and Kashmir.

The text of the Jammu and Kashmir Act, along with the Bommai Committee's approach paper to democratic decentralisation are appended for reference. The latter document will place the future of panchayati raj in all the States in the proper perspective against the backdrop of the emerging issues of devolution of power *vis*-a-*vis* the nature of our polity.

The Government of Jammu and Kashmir must give utmost priority to implementation of this Act. That will show its faith in the people. Who wins or who loses the elections is immaterial. Setting the political process in motion is the crux of the matter. And that too must be done in such a manner that the people's faith in the democratic process is strengthened. It should usher in a new era of people's participation in the political process.

GEORGE MATHEW

ONE

Reflections on Panchayati Raj

S K Dey

WHERE in the whole world has Nature created such a place as Kashmir? Look at the eyes of the ordinary man who struggles to get timber for fire. His eyes shine. There is nothing that is lacking for the people to be totally happy and composed. Individually as well as collectively. Yet, there is poverty. Why?

Since the beginning of the history of our Independence and our development, what we wanted to carry out in common, I do not know. If the Chief Minister has done the absolutely right thing, I don't want to question it. I am totally disturbed. I have been to Kashmir since 1934. I have visited Jammu also. As a person who has seen through Kashmir for 54 years, I have wondered why there is so much poverty in the State.

I was sitting here quietly, listening and wondering within myself. This Dal Lake, I have stayed here also, before 1947 in house boats. The Dal Lake was totally clear and undisturbed except with four trees in a small island, and then this road which went via the Raj Bhavan to the Nishat Garden and the Shalimar Garden. Now a new structure has come up here. I have not been in Kashmir for the past 15 years or so. I was invited by Bhagwan Sahay, the then Governor. He was retiring and he asked me to stay with him for a fortnight before he left Kashmir. So I came here and stayed with him, and I saw something of Kashmir at that time. It has changed. The lake view has changed and I find something has come up here. I have known the whole of India very intimately, as very few people have. I have had the opportunity as Minister for Community Development to travel across India as far as I wanted, as deeply as I wanted. We sit here in this Sher-e-Kashmir convention hall, the like of which does not exist anywhere else in the country, including perhaps the Vigyan Bhavan. This whole structure here is very comfortable for this meeting. I have been asking myself, sitting here, who constructed this? Who provided the material, technology and other things that were required? Who harnessed these for the construction of this complex? I have no answer other than to say that the labour and sweat of the people of this whole land had made it.

What is panchayati raj? Believe me, I do not feel like talking about it any more. I feel like conversing with people who mean business and there are very few people who mean business. Individual business, yes. I am sorry to say, it is difficult to find people who take seriously collective business of life as a whole — collective business of the people of their own village, of their own district, of their own State.

You ask people about panchayati raj — "Panchayati Raj, my God! It has failed". The Cooperative Sahkari Samaj — they say it has all collapsed. Community development? It has also failed. A wonderful tribute to our own conscience. I am totally disturbed, and I feel I should talk to you about where we began in the early '50s and why we began. No one else can talk about it at this length.

So, in 1952, Jawaharlal Nehru asked me, "We have struggled fifty, sixty, seventy years for liberating this country from foreign rule. For what purpose? To make the people the rulers. I want you to get the key from me. Relieve me of the burden of this chair". Every villager began to think and joined his countrymen in the villages to think together, run together, to do what he wished, develop his own resources. And so the Community development programme originated.

On 11, 12 and 13 May 1952, there was a conference of the development commissioners of the States. The entire Cabinet of the Government of India came. I was appointed the administrator. I was paid Re One a month as salary. I had said the resources were enough to support myself and I didn't want to take anything more from the Government, therefore, I continued like this for about nine years. When I had exhausted everything—well that is a different story.

As administrator I was asked to talk to the development commissioners in the presence of the Cabinet members from my heart, just as I had wanted to. Well, believe me, I do not know what I said. I come from a very poor village joint family of 19 members. We had five acres of land, wet land. I have known poverty, the likes of which very few people have. I had to educate myself. Fortunately, I got a scholarship from primary school onwards and I also had education up to my master of science degree in electrical engineering. Now, I wanted to develop my own village, eradicate the poverty by becoming an engineer and I became an engineer. I thought I would earn money and develop my village. It never worked. It is not one village that must be developed. The country has to develop all the villages.

Well, I discussed this point with Jawaharlal Nehru. He said, "Yes, I give you all the 5,57,000 villages. Go, and tell them they are the masters. Let them do whatever they wish to do with this country". Jawaharlal Nehru inaugurated this meeting after my mad address. Can you imagine the position of the Prime Minister who is addressed in this manner by a complete savage like me? It is a great embarrassment to himself and everybody else. He tried to excuse himself and save me from embarrassment and said, "You know, the administrator has spoken. I felt in him the tension of an adventure and that is what I wish to propagate to this country. That there is a tension of adventure and everyone must activate oneself".

We are here now to discuss to extend that tension of adventurer to the entire country. And give the keys of ruling, administering and developing themselves to the people. That is the problem and I believe, that is the problem of panchayati raj. We started. I came to Kashmir years ago and met Sheikh Abdullah for the first time. Nehru had told me that he is a person I would not find a likeness of anywhere. He said, "Meet him. He is quite well versed, an intellectual giant". I also met Ghulam Mohammed, a living dynamo. We wanted to spread the fire of progress all over India and thought that if we began with Jammu and Kashmir at the top, the fire would travel downwards throughout the country. Thus, the panchayati raj programme was launched in the northernmost State. You will be surprised to know that 1,000 panchayat ghars were built in a few months. Other institutions were created along with these.

Permit me to digress here for a while.

I used to walk with a stick which I learnt to use since my childhood because walking through villages at night without a stick is dangerous. There are jackals, wild dogs and snakes against which you have to safeguard yourself. So, I still carry my stick. It has become a habit. In the past I have told people in Kashmir that when they talk of development, I am afraid of leaving my stick here by mistake. Because, six months later when I come here and look for my stick, I find it has grown into a tree. This is the soil of this State. You can grow anything here. You have everything in Jammu and Kashmir.

Now the question arises about implementation of the programmes of agriculture, horticulture, sericulture, road building, irrigation, soil conservation, health care, education, arts and crafts development, women's upliftment, child welfare and recreation. Soon, it was realised that you cannot run a programme of development with the initiative of only Government officers. Of course they have done an exceptionally good job. The development commissioners and the collectors (as district development officers), with some minor exceptions, did exceptionally good work. The block development officers, the technical officers and the top civil service officers left an impression permanently in my mind that government employees, if they are given an opportunity can rise to the occasion by their honesty, integrity, initiative and the urge to motivate people to put in their mite to the development effort. This is the conclusion I derive after working with Government employees over a period of 25 years. They have never failed me. But so many realised that the initiative of Government employees alone does not suffice. We require institutions of people themselves for development and administrative purposes, for panchayati raj institutions at the village, block and district levels. People's involvement is also necessary for the working of cooperative societies from villages to the districts and up to the State level and then up to the national level in the form of federations. Now, this also was started in Jammu and Kashmir as well as in the rest of India.

The politically elected representation in the State legislature as well as the Parliament permitted me to carry out the programmes in close collaboration with the Centre and the States. We had a consultative committee of Parliamentary members and you will be surprised to know that of the 700 members in the Rajya Sabha and Lok Sabha, we had as many as 150 members in our consultative committee. This was the first such committee created in India in 1964. I had to divide it into three groups — one for panchayati raj, one for sahkari samaj and one for community development. This was done because you cannot have meetings of more than 50 people who wish real participation. And the problem I referred to earlier, resolve around participation — people's participation. For they are the real guardians and holders of power in this country. Do they really participate with the Government? Do they lead the Government? If the people do not lead the Government, then the Government will try to lead the people. It is a very vital question in panchayati raj — who wants the people to guide, the panchayats and panchayati institutions? Or should the panchayati institutions ask participation of the people?

Participation can mean just speaking to the people, as politicians speak, as I have spoken and I am speaking. But that is not participation. Participation means an active involvement of the people in implementation of everything pertaining to the development and welfare of the community. And these include community development, economic development, social development and administrative development — all these taken together. And panchayati raj was conceptualised keeping this in view. As Jawaharlal Nehru said, "it was power to the people". What did Gandhi say about it? According to Nehru, "Gandhi said: 'My conception of swaraj is not the concentration of authority in a few, but the acquisition of the capacity in the many'." Now, I think this should be written in golden letters, and that is what Jawaharlal Nehru wanted: to see the enlightening of the village people to take the rule in their own hands, rather than talking and participating in discussions with the Government. But the elected leaders began to complain. They said: "in the past when we used to go for election, Bapuji would say: 'Take the nation ahead, educate the people, bring them together, move forward.' Now when we meet Bapuji, he asks: 'Who are you? I had sent you as an elected representative five years ago, but for five years I haven't seen your face. Our village level work, our community development programme, have all been wasted'." Ask any elected representative of the people. Ask him to touch his heart and tell you what he feels about panchayati raj. He despises it, I am sorry to say. After Jawaharlal Nehru's death one hoped that the country would have thought how best it would make the people the real owners and guides of the nation. But did this happen?

Soon after Nehru's death a new legislation was passed on panchayati raj. I was told that the implementation of panchayati raj would mean that I would have to abolish community development bodies all over the country. I found then that I had no constituency of my own. I had a constituency from where I got elected but that did not help me at all. My constituency was Jawaharlal Nehru. But he was gone. Questions came up in Parliament in spite of me. One day at least 50 members stood up in the Lok Sabha and said: "The community development programme has been abolished. The agencies have been abolished in Madhya Pradesh. We want to know when this ministry (Community Development) is going to be abolished?" This is on record in Parliament. I was absolutely stunned. Imagine, not one person stood up to say, don't do this. Later, I accosted Prime Minister Lal Bahadur Shastri as he was going back to his room in Parliament House and said, "Lal Bahadurji, I wish to get out of all this. Panditji is not here and you sat there silently while I was being hammered and the entire Parliament said that the Community Development Ministry should be abolished. You did not say anything. I want to get out of it right away". He said: "Aye Dey Sahab, you don't understand anything. The problem is that you don't understand the public. Our Parliament is also a kind of public. I want to tell you one simple truth. Jawaharlal Nehru had great faith in them (the people). He thought they could always rule. Even Jawaharlal Nehru didn't understand people fully. Can they run a district and a panchayat? They will destroy it. But I didn't want to say all this then otherwise people would say that I sit in Jawaharlal Nehru's chair and in the end his most important programme, to bring the people together and hand over the keys to let them rule, remains unfulfilled. We will sit and try to provide them help but we will not rule them. I will call a Congress working committee meeting and seek advice from the leaders, and if they say that there have to be some changes in the programme, I will do it and people will be happy. See, you can understand my point".

I wondered what kind of theory he was trying to expound. I told him, "A villager can become the Prime Minister of India and run this country and even sell it if he wishes to. Do you mean to say that a sarpanch cannot run a village with village people living around him — the very people who elected him? A district level chief, the president of a zilla parishad, cannot run a district? Of course, he can come to the Centre, become a minister, become the Prime Minister. Is that the theory you are trying to propagate?" He replied, "Aye Dey Sahab, what a theory you have made. Leave all this to me. Leave it. No use in arguing". Well, I realised Jawaharlal Nehru's days were over. I recall, just a few days before he passed away in 1964, Jawaharlal called me at midnight. I found him in a very contemplative mood when I drove over to his Teen Murti Bhawan residence. His head was bent as he looked at me and said, "Look, I want to ask you a question. Suppose the entire Government holds against your community development programme and panchayati raj, will you be able to resist?" I said, "Today they won't do so and the reason is that in the entire Hindi-speaking belt, panchayati raj is a facade. But we have some States which are doing very well". I said that whether it was Maharashtra or Gujarat the programme cannot be abolished, though they can be dislocated or disturbed. But in five years, I think, we will be able to abolish them or disturb them unduly, I added. He said, "Look my friend, sorry, you have no time. There is no time. Panchayati raj cannot be saved, nor even your programme".

I have already narrated what transpired in Parliament a few months after Jawaharlal passed away. Then after some time, the Indira Government came to power. She, with one stroke abolished the only ministry of its kind in the world. The words 'community development' have been abolished from usage and have now been replaced by the term, 'rural development'. And that had had no ministry. It is a department of agriculture at the headquarters of India and the staff has been increased considerably. But they do not know what is happening in community development, rural development or panchayati raj, or even in the cooperatives. But the staff has increased and the force has increased. Now, we are having a seminar here discussing panchayati raj. I don't know whether there is any member of the Central Government dealing with panchayati government or community development today who is present here. Now, that speaks for itself. Well, the Indira Government abolished it and nobody raised a word. Even the press would say that community development has failed. If you ask a citizen, the elite, they say community development has failed. It is rural development which is succeeding. Previously, we had the coordination of all the nation-building departments. Now, they call it the IRDP (Integrated Rural Development Programme). So, it is a different programme. You can use the English language in whatever way you want.

While all this talk of panchayati raj is going on in the country, one wonders if there is any genuine intention of evolving rural self-government and all-round development. Looking at the emerging trends it would appear as if the foremost aim of the country is to have a five-star culture, as is growing with a vengeance in the world today? I travelled across the whole world on behalf of the United

Nations, after I ceased to be a minister. I have seen what is happening in Africa, Latin America and West Asia. Rural people are streaming into the metropolitan cities in an endless flow in developing nations throughout the world. At the end of the mission I gave the UN a report, titled, 'But, for Whom?' They were completely puzzled. The UN people said that they had never heard of a consultant submitting a report with a question mark in the title. My thesis applied to the entire UN system, the power of organisation at the world level, in dislocating national coordination, because its members were pulling apart just as departments at the State level pull apart. Therefore, we should ask ourselves this question, I told them: Whom are we dealing with? With the middle class? Or are we meddling with the people? The whole of Latin America is an example. And my report on Latin America was titled, 'To Nations with Nation'. But this was in 1968. Today we are in 1988. What happened in Latin America was the worst that could have happened in human history, thanks to America's participation in development under the doctrine which gave them the exclusive opportunity to deal with South American nations.

Coming back to our discussion about India, I find that our country is not just two nations, but something immeasurably worse. Look at the five-star hotels that have come up in Delhi. I have stayed till Independence in two of the best hotels, the Oberoi Maidens and the Imperial. I paid Rs. 14 per day for board and lodging. Today the minimum charge in a five-star hotel is Rs. 1,000 without food and it is not only foreigners who are staying in these hotels. There are many Indians as well. Even an ordinary head clerk of an ordinary organisation is not content when he comes to Delhi unless he lives in a five-star hotel. All this luxury in the midst of grinding poverty. Look at the *jhuggi* colony near my house. People living without water, electricity or proper shelter in squalour and dirt for generations. And there are around 25 million people living in *jhuggies* all over Delhi. This is Delhi, our capital city!

Srinagar too has undergone changes. It has no skyscrapers, of course, thank God! It is very peaceful. People are moving but not as a crowd in a rush, not collectively but individually to meet others. But life is not so for everyone here. Not a day passes without newspaper reports about a raid here or there. We are going through a culture which is totally uprooting us, the middle class.

Nature in her terrific abundance has given Jammu and Kashmir everything this State requires. I say it is not a sin only but a crime for any pocket of poverty to exist here. A Kashmiri is an excellent worker. Look at his eyes, his intelligence. He can compare with anybody in India. He has everything that he wants by way of the climatic conditions. How do we make him free of hunger and deprivation? Can it be done by a Government? It can be done only by themselves. That I think is the aim of panchayati raj. Now you cannot have panchayati raj unless you have the people's cooperation. Panchayati raj cannot deal with economic problems without people's cooperation. Therefore, you have to have a different kind of institution for looking after the economic aspects of the matter. For that you have to think of Sahkari Samaj. And when you talk of Kashmir, the biggest industrial base is horticulture. Have you developed this?

When you talk of panchayati raj, it is an institution you are creating while unleashing a process of people getting together intelligently to think of their common future, economic as well as social. It is an unending process of reconciliation and working together not for individual gain but for a collective purpose. If this can happen at the ground level it will automatically work at the State level. Of course, I am fully aware of the problem involved but as Jawaharlal Nehru said, "I only want an answer. You have a village school, a village panchayat, and a village cooperative society. When you have these three institutions you should carry the country forward".

TWO

Towards Strengthening India's Federal Democracy

Nirmal K. Mukarji

THE State of Jammu and Kashmir has a position in the Indian federal system closest to what scholars regard as classical federalism. It has its own Constitution but has joined the Indian Union through a compact enshrined in the national Constitution. This State thus gives on a unique window from which to survey the federal scene in the country.

One recalls with admiration the statesmanship displayed by men like Pandit Nehru and Sheikh Abdullah in devising a highly innovatory provision like Article 370. Not only did this enable Jammu and Kashmir to become an honoured member of the Indian Union despite being alone in having its own Constitution, it also provided an opening through which the State could gradually enlarge its participation in the national polity. One cannot help noticing that this much-discussed article, located as it is in a section largely dealing with special provisions for individual States, paved the way for some remarkable federal engineering undertaken to solve the problems of other States. The next ten articles, Articles 371 to 371-I, contain special provisions for such diverse States as Maharashtra, Gujarat, Nagaland, Assam, Manipur, Andhra Pradesh, Sikkim, Mizoram, Arunachal Pradesh and Goa. In each case there was a problem to which the national response was to arrive at a State-specific compact and fit that into the Constitution. This group of articles reflects, in a small but significant manner, the diversity of the country and the corresponding flexibility displayed in providing for this diversity without damaging the basic features of the Constitution.

What this shows is that the federal side of the polity has not remained static. A more telling illustration of this is the creative use of Article 3 which permits the formation of new States and the reshaping of existing ones. It is unusual for a federal system to have units which are destructible. The measure was conceived in the context of 500-odd princely States needing to be assimilated after Independence, but it has proved useful in other situations which arose later. It is not necessary to trace in detail how the present configuration of States has evolved. There was, first, the incorporation of the aforesaid princely States which resulted in the country being parcelled into Parts A, B, C and D States. There was, next, the demand triggered by Andhra Pradesh for recognition of the linguistic principle, which led to a comprehensive and largely durable reorganisation of State boundaries. Third, the grant of full statehood to a relatively small territory like Nagaland initiated a course in which, on tribal or other grounds, several other small States came into being. The political map of India bears hardly any resemblance to what the British left behind. It cannot be said that the number of States will stay at the present 25.

II

Five years ago I wrote an article on *The Future of Federalism in India (Newstime,* 12/13 February 1984), from which I quote:

> "Different types of federations abound in the world; some formed to create a centre — as in the USA . . ., others to disperse the centre as in our own country; some democratic, others authoritarian (e.g., in UAE or the USSR); some with few constituents, others with many. All federations keep changing with the times, sometimes by formal amendments of their constitution, but most often through the evolution of new conventions, agreements and styles of functioning. There is no single ideal federal system, a point missed by those who plead for 'genuine' or 'true' federalism. There is, however, always a gap between a federal system as it *has* evolved up to a point of time and as it

should have evolved having regard to the changed situation. This is because objective circumstances change much faster than the ability of the system to adapt to them."

I propose to take this as my starting point and explore the issues that arise from the above observations. What are the major changes that have taken place in the objective circumstances in India? And what modifications do these call for in the country's system of governance? But before these can be fruitfully discussed it is necessary to clear the decks in regard to two preliminary matters.

First, is India just another country? In a cultural-historical sense every country in the world is unique. But India's uniqueness does not lie only in its culture, which is extraordinarily rich, or in its history, which is extraordinarily long. There are more tangible factors which mark it out. One is size. India is, after all, one of the largest countries of the world. Population-wise, and when we are talking of systems of governance it is people who count, it is in the same bracket as China, one being a little over a billion and the other a little under. The next bracket comprises the USSR and the USA, both with populations well under half a billion each. Billionaire countries have their own problems of governance which are unusually difficult to solve. Precedents from elsewhere, even from the countries in the nearest bracket, are not of much avail.

The other marker of India's uniqueness is its diversity. So much has been written on this that one needs to pick out only the more significant threads. There is the shameful phenomenon of Harijans who are classified as Hindus for census purposes but are in fact treated as the dregs of society, never to be allowed to come through the impermeable barrier of social sanctions that sets them apart and down. There is the devil of communalism. In China, Buddhists, Confucians, Muslims and others live together in peace and there is no communal problem. Not so in India. Here, Hindus and Muslims have been unable to find a *modus vivendi*, even after partition. There is the mosaic of linguistic and tribal peoples, each grounded in its own territorial space. China has territory-linked ethnic groups on its borders but over 90 per cent of Chinese are Hans with common language and common script. India, on the other hand, is a patchwork quilt of territory-based groups each with its own language and often with its own script.

Size-wise, China and India stand at the top amongst the countries of the world. Diversity-wise, India is far more complex than China. This has always been the case, but like in a mile-race the front-runner pulls ahead in the last lap, India chose to become a democracy when it became independent and thus underlined its uniqueness. So India is not just another country. Its size, diversity and democratic commitment characterise it as pre-eminently unique. This plain fact needs to be borne in mind not as something to boast about but as something to worry over when considering the various problems of governance that beset this country. There is no place for petty thinking when faced with continental magnitudes and unmatched diversity.

Second, while there is no question that we are a democracy, are we a federal system at all? The Constitution makers deliberately chose to describe India as a Union of States, rejecting amendments suggesting that the word 'Federal' should be put before the word 'Union' or the word 'Federation' should replace the word 'Union'. They also consciously opted for a strong Centre and gave overriding legislative, administrative and financial powers to the Union Government. Nehru explained to the Constituent Assembly that, when partition was a settled fact, it would be injurious to the interest of the country to provide for a weak Central authority which would be incapable of ensuring peace, of coordinating vital matters of common concern and of speaking effectively for the whole country in the international sphere. In practice also, the Congress which ruled at the Centre as well as in all the States for most of the first two decades after Independence, simply carried on the "command" system of governance where the British left off. Ambedkar's remark that the country was an integral whole and that its people lived under a single *imperium*, acquires significance when one learns that the Latin word "imperium" means 'command' or 'dominion'. A strong Centre in law and a command system in practice conditioned people into thinking that India had adopted an essentially unitary system.

There is, however, another side to the picture. While the use of the word 'federal' was avoided and a strong Centre created, the Constitution did at the same time delimit the legislative and administrative domains of the Centre and the States. Again, while arguing against a weak Central authority, Nehru also stated that the soundest framework for our Constitution was a *federation* with a strong Centre. Ambedkar further clarified that the Constitution as it emerged from the Constituent Assembly in 1949 was unitary in extraordinary situations, such as war (or emergency), but *federal in normal times*. When non-Congress governments began appearing in 1967, the command system could not obviously continue to operate. This was acknowledged in the President's address to the newly elected Parliament in the following words: "For the first time since Independence, governments of political complexion different from that of the government at the Centre have been formed in several States. In a *federal polity,* this is to be expected. Our Constitution has provisions defining and regulating the relationship between the Union and the States and their mutual obligations". A foreign scholar dubbed the Indian Constitution as quasi-federal, presumably treating the USA system as the norm. However, as rightly pointed out by the Sarkaria Commission, these labels hardly matter as the levels of government in India derive their respective powers from a written Constitution.

The conclusion is inescapable that in law, as Nehru said, India is a federation with a strong Centre. In practice, the federal dimension lay dormant during the first two decades of Congress hegemony but began asserting itself in the '80s when non-Congress governments with stable majorities were formed in about a third of the country. The Sarkaria Commission appointed to examine Centre-State relations emphasised the need for more cooperative federalism. Therefore the answer to the question whether we are a federal system is 'yes' in law albeit with a strong Centre, but 'not yet' in practice though moving in that direction. We are in fact a federal democracy.

III

Foremost among the changes in objective circumstances that have taken place in the country are demographic changes. From about 350 million at Independence, India's population has gone up to above 800 million and is projected to cross the billion mark at the turn of the century. The age pyramid remains as flat as ever, which means that in absolute numbers, the young comprise more than half the total population. People are moving into the cities in larger numbers owing to a combination of pull and push factors. Urban population was about 60 million at Independence, rose to 160 million in 1981 and is projected to be 360 million in the year 2001. More than a third of all Indians will be living in cities when that 'glorious' twenty-first century dawns, as against a sixth when we became independent. Economists, planners and the intelligentsia generally rate these demographic realities negatively. There is no question that there is genuine cause for alarm. Much, though not all, of the alarm stems from a view that large numbers of people, especially when many of them are young and often aggressively demanding, constitute a liability. If people were to be thought of as human resource and therefore a potential asset, the alarm bells might be less clangorous. Liability or asset, the sheer magnitude of the numbers places a question mark on whether a largely static system of governance can cope with the rapidly expanding demographic reality.

Next are the changes brought about by political development. The Central legislature we started with, which also doubled as the Constituent Assembly, was elected in 1946. The size of the electorate then in the whole of undivided India, excluding the princely States, was 35 million. Then came Article 326 which provided for universal adult suffrage, perhaps the most impactful clause of the Constitution. As a result the electorate for the first general election held in 1952 jumped five-fold to 173 million. The figure went up to 250 million in 1967 and 364 million in 1984. With the voting age lowered to 18, it will exceed 450 million for the next general election. The change from restricted to universal franchise thus meant moving from elite to mass politics. If the masses had remained politically quiescent there would have been little difference. But frequent and regular elections served as schools of political education, steadily raising the level of political consciousness. The successful overthrow of entrenched regimes in several States and even at the Centre had the effect of accelerating the process of politicisation. While literacy crawled from 16.7 per cent in 1951 to 36.2 per cent in 1981, political education leapt ahead. Given India's powerful word-to-mouth tradition, the written word was not needed for political issues to be discussed at teashops across the country with earthy wisdom.

Changes wrought by economic development are a mixed bag. On the one hand, the country has become nearly self-sufficient in foodgrains. The threat of widespread famine has gone and in fact the possibility has opened for food security measures to be undertaken here and there, like the provision of subsidised rice to the poor in Andhra Pradesh. Indian industry now produces a wide range of products. Infrastructural areas like power, transport and irrigation have registered good progress, thanks mainly to the public sector. On the other hand, the overall growth rate of the economy until the end of the '70s averaged a mere 3.7 per cent per annum, which having regard to population increase meant only 1.5 per cent per capita. In the '80s, growth is claimed to have gone past this "Hindu rate", as the late Prof Raj Krishna called it, and touched 5 per cent. But much of the increase is accounted for by "drone" items of the service sector, like the bureaucracy and defence. More disturbing is the spread of economic benefits. The top 20 per cent take nearly half of the Gross National Product, against which the bottom 20 per cent are left with only 7 per cent. Economic development has created glaring disparity between the rich and the poor. The poor comprise not only the bottom 40 per cent or less, going by official definitions, but in fact all those other than the top 20 per cent, that is four-fifths of the population or 650 million people.

The picture that emerges from these dimensions of change is one of a vast and growing population advancing rapidly in political consciousness but being made increasingly aware that the fruits of economic growth, meagre as they are, are not for them but for a chosen few. There are numerous signals that the imbalance between expectations and satisfactions, a familiar enough phenomenon in most societies, is driving individuals and groups outside the system of governance into an extra-Constitutional polity. We need to think whether and how the system can be given more stretch and flexibility to cope with discontent. But before that some of the major changes in the political arena need to be noted.

The most significant is the decline of the once-great Congress party. In a sense the decline started when Congress came into office, for power began to corrupt. By the time the Nehru era ended, the rot had begun to set in, creating room for non-Congressism of three types to arise: Left Fronts, self-respect movements like the DMK and Lohia-inspired opposition unity moves to ensure one-to-one electoral contests. The net result was that, in the 1967 general election, Congress was ousted from power in eight States. This became a turning point. One the one hand, democracy received a shot in the arm because alternatives to Congress were seen to be a possibility. On the other, a shocked Congress unleashed a formidable backlash. First, most of the newly formed non-Congress governments were swept aside. Next, since the States had proved to be vulnerable, extraordinary measures were adopted to centralise power. On the party side, there was a split with the faction in power adopting the 'fuehrer' model, doing away with intra-party elections. On the government side, huge para-military forces were created. The reach of the Intelligence Bureau was extended right across the country and especially to States which persisted with non-Congressism. President's Rule began to be imposed more frequently. Economic management and planning were so conducted as to make States increasingly dependent on the Centre. Captains of industry, czars of science and technology and indeed all those most favoured by the pattern of development, went along happily. The political and economic 'haves' thus made common cause to make the government of the country more centralised than Nehru or anyone else had ever visualised. This was a far cry from the federal democracy the country had opted for.

Correspondingly significant is the rise of countervailing forces. If the benefits of economic development went largely to the top 20 per cent, the gains of political development quietly accrued to the rest of the people. Elite groups corrupted the electoral system to keep themselves in and the masses out. However, when centralisation culminated in the Emergency, the masses voted the offending regime out at the first opportunity. They did the same to the successor regime when that failed them. Congress wrongly interpreted this as a mandate for renewed centralisation and paid for this by losing State after State in a series of elections. Non-Congress elements in the States joined hands to demand that the federal structure of the Constitution, overshadowed for long by the command system of the Congress, be restored and strengthened. Federal reform thus came on the national agenda. Meanwhile, the Left Front in West Bengal innovated a bold programme of land reform coupled with vitalisation of panchayats. For the first time since Independence, the masses in that State felt the glow of freedom through active participation in panchayat self-governance. What distinguished West Bengal's panchayats from earlier versions was that they were openly political in character. Karnataka and Andhra Pradesh, which too had non-Congress governments, also transformed their panchayats into politically elected units of self-government. The concept of panchayat governments pioneered by these States caught the imagination of the country. Decentralisation below the State level through devolution of political power to panchayat governments thus became an important adjunct of the movement for federal reform.

IV

The above analysis of changing circumstances points to the need for federal reform and for decentralisation below the State level. Since 'federal reform' is a euphemism for decentralisation from the Centre to the States, the single agenda that stands out is decentralisation. This may be viewed as a cascade descending from the Centre to the States and from the States to sub-State levels. If the cascade stops at the first stage, the States would be choked with powers and functions, and people's participation would remain a far cry. If, on the other hand, the cascade only starts at the second stage, the States are unlikely to part with enough powers and functions to make sub-State levels viable for fear that this may reduce their importance too much. All the past experiments to decentralise below the State level, especially variants of panchayati raj, have suffered on this account. The States must therefore receive as well as give. Decentralisation confined to the States-downward stage does not make sense and is doomed to fail. The cascade must start at the Union level and go all the way down, stage by stage.

The critical element is finance. It may be stated as a proposition, at least in the Indian context, that functions go where there is money, regardless of constitutional lists. Therefore, when thinking of decentralisation, there will have to be a new financial regime as between the Centre, the States and the districts. On the one hand, the Centre must be left with resources to meet its essential obligations. On the other, the States and the districts, not being in a position to raise adequate resources of their own, must have the oxygen of assured, united devolution of funds from the Centre in sufficient measure to make purposeful self-government at these levels possible. So far the percentage shares of the States in the central taxes have been determined by the Finance Commissions. Dr Raja Chelliah, the noted expert in public finance, once urged the need for finality in this matter. Specifically, he suggested that 40 per cent of income-tax and corporation tax and 35 per cent of Union excises should go to the States and in addition 5 per cent of income-tax and corporation tax to local bodies, and that a provision to this effect should be made in the Constitution. The Finance Commission should thereafter only distribute the total of the States' share among the States. On the grants side, Dr Chelliah suggested that all block and other grants should be channelled mainly through the Finance

Commissions (rather than the Planning Commission), which should be guided not by the gap-filling approach but by well-accepted principles of equalisation. As regards loans, he wrote that "the basis of allocation of market borrowing among the States needs to be examined and new principles have to be evolved".

Going beyond Dr. Chelliah's refreshing approach, one is inclined to suggest (as a non-expert) that, in order to introduce finality and avoid recriminatory debate, a provision may be made in the Constitution that 45 per cent of the aggregate resources of the Centre (leaving aside obviously unshareable items like provident funds of Central employees) should go to the States, of which 5 per cent should be earmarked for being passed on to the districts. The Centre's aggregate resources are of two kinds, non-loan and loan. Non-loan resources (45 per cent) should go to the States and districts as unconditional devolutions. Loan resources (45 per cent) including market borrowing, external borrowing and deficit financing, should also be devolved unconditionally except for normal loan terms. Devolution of market borrowing should be by allocating ceilings within which major States should do their own borrowing, while the Centre may do so on behalf of the minor States. Finance Commissions would then be left with the twin task of determining the shareable aggregate resources of the Union, non-loan and loan, and distributing the shares of the States and districts among the States, eschewing the gap-filling approach and adopting equalisation principles. Within the States, at least the major ones, there would have to be State finance commissions which do a similar job in respect of the districts. The States should be required to set aside 5 per cent of their own aggregate resources (excluding devolutions from the Centre) for devolution to the districts. These and the earmarked devolutions from the Centre would comprise the distributable pool for the districts.

There must also be a new planning regime. We need to find a way to federalise national planning. The Planning Commission should move out of the investment-cum-growth type of planning in which it has remained locked and move into the hitherto almost unexplored terrain of policy planning. It should think anew about issues like the reasons for persistent mass poverty and deprivation, the reasons for the continued backwardness of regions, the roots of public unrest of various kinds, the oppression to which the weak are subjected, the decline of institutions like the police and judicial administration, the status of women, the proper nurturing and education of children, the full implications of population growth, the proper management of water and land resources, the restructuring of relations with neighbouring countries, the impact of external policies, the proper balance between defence and development, the rising cost of the bureaucracy, and many others. It should seek to build national consensus on the policies which the country as a whole should adopt in regard to such issues. The Commission may involve itself in sectoral planning for Central subjects. For the rest, planning should be decentralised to the States and districts. The States for sure and, to the maximum extent possible, the districts too must strengthen their planning capabilities. Vigorous State and district planning, within the compass of nationally accepted policies and under a financial regime which permits local innovations, would be the way to harmonise the planning idea with the federal.

The Constitution-makers provided for elected governments at the Centre and in the States but strangely left the inherited 'district officer' system untouched in the districts. Strangely, because local self-government was on the agenda of the freedom movement long before *purna swaraj* and yet it came to be overlooked. Whatever the reasons for this, the objective situation now calls for a review. On the one hand, today's district officer has far too much to do and this means that he is unable to do anything effectively enough. On the other, the political awakening of the people has led them to expect much more from the system than it can deliver. Instead of flogging 'district officer' rule any longer, the time is ripe to consider letting the people run their own affairs through elected governments in the districts. Decentralisation below the State level must take the democratic route of devolution to these governments.

If such governments are not to go the way of panchayati raj institutions (PRIs), they must possess characteristics, the lack of which led to the failure of the latter. District governments must be recognised as political entities, with political parties openly contesting elections. The past approach of keeping panchayats sanitised from politics, though well intentioned in one sense, overlooked the invigorating role of politics as an engine for change. It also deprived the polity of an entry stage for new recruits into politics and a nursery for grooming such entrants for higher responsibilities. Without the political dimension there can be no real democracy. And anything short of genuine democracy will perish just as surely as guided democracy did elsewhere or party-less democracy in the case of the first generation PRIs. The second generation PRIs, having remedied matters in this respect, stand out as useful precedents.

Further, district governments must look after the totality of district governance, with the district bureaucracy coming squarely under them. The division between regulatory and developmental functions, initiated by community development and continued in PRIs, is artificial and untenable. It compels development to stay within the limits set by the present societal configuration. This is so because any attempt to change the configuration, such as through land reform, inevitably comes up against the power structure. When that happens, regulatory administration all too often sides with the power elite. If there is to be any worthwhile change, this collusion must go, and that can only become possible if the two arms, regulatory and developmental, are required to work together under district governments. Ultimately, what matters is who wields the *lathi* and if that remains with the district officer, district governments will be just as unable to deliver genuine development as PRIs.

Also, the fate of district governments must not be left to the tender mercies of State governments. This means two things. One, elections must be held at regular intervals under the overall supervision of the Election Commission. As far as possible, the method of elections should be direct because the indirect route is easily manipulable. Two, supersessions should be barred. In the case of the States there is the controversial and much misused Article 356 under which elected State governments can be removed and President's Rule imposed in the event of failure of the constitutional machinery. Sooner or later this vestige of colonial rule will have to go. In respect of the districts, there is no justification for replicating a measure which would give State governments a handle to remove inconvenient district governments.

Lastly, district governments must be nested in the federal idea, forming a third tier of the polity. The third tier would subsume self governing units at sub-district levels right down to the *gram sabhas*. This again means two things. One, that 'The Districts' must find a place in the Constitution, not perhaps in the elaborate manner of Part VI dealing with 'The States' but equally not in the perfunctory manner of Part VIII dealing with 'The Union Territories'. Two, the introduction of a third tier must not squeeze the intermediate second tier or be seen as attempting to do so. If the aim is to strengthen and enlarge India's federal democracy, it is as important to make the States more effective as to carve out a third tier for the districts. Consequently, a reordering of Centre-State relations must go hand in hand with extending the federal idea to a third tier. As of now, the Centre has overburdened itself with functions pertaining to State subjects. If the superfluous fat were to be shed, the Centre might handle what remains better, and the States would have more to share out with the districts.

It would be a pity if democratic decentralisation, for which as a concept there is wide support, resulted only in making incremental improvements in panchayati raj within the existing framework of governance. It should mean a fundamentally new system of governance through two inter-connected measures: a new scheme of relations between the Centre, the States and the districts, based on optional decentralisation; and a third tier of democratic district governments to replace bureaucratic 'district officer' rule. At the end of the day, the genuineness of democratic decentralisation will have to be subjected to two tests. Has the machinery of government at the Centre and in the States visibly shrunk in terms of fewer ministers, fewer departments and generally smaller bureaucracies? And has it been possible to wind up colonial dispensation of 'district officer' rule? If these tests remain unsatisfied, the 'revolution' in the system of governance will have to wait for another day.

THREE

Political Parties in Panchayati Raj

George Mathew

WHETHER and to what extent political parties should participate in panchayati raj election is a question that has occupied centre stage of the discussions on panchayati raj in the country even before Independence. In fact the Santhanam Committee (1964) on panchayati raj elections had stated that one of the most controversial issues they had to deal with was the above question.[1] The question had added significance because of the two prominent, at the same time sharply divided, schools of thought on the subject of political parties' participation in local bodies elections. One major line of thought advocated apolitical panchayat bodies and the other was against the "woolly idea of having local bodies' elections on an apolitical basis".[2]

The Jammu and Kashmir Panchayati Act, 1989 does not say anything about political parties' participation in elections. For that matter constitutions need not say anything about parties unless proportional representation is provided as for instance, in the Constitution of West Germany. In the Constitution of India, parties are mentioned only in terms of the anti-defection clause. The Constitution 64th Amendment Bill introduced with fanfare by the Congress(I) government in the Lok Sabha in April 1989 had defined "Panchayat" as an institution of self-government. However, in the context of opposing schools of thought regarding political parties' participation in the 'governments' below the State level and the not-too-favourable attitude of a major party like the Congress(I) on the subject, this paper attempts to discuss the 'route' of this debate and argue that without official participation of political parties, the panchayats will be democracy in form only, without content.

The Sarvodaya ideas, inspired by Gandhiji was that PRIs should be "non-political", meaning that political parties should be kept out. Consensus was considered the best way of arriving at decisions. Jayaprakash Narayan believed that parties corrupted the whole of the panchayati raj programme and used decentralisation for selfish party interests. Sarvodayees wanted to rebuild Indian democracy on the basis of Gram Samaj at the bottom and upper tiers at the Samiti, district, State and all-India levels. Representation at each level must be through indirect elections. They believed that by this, the principle of consensus, if not unanimity, will prevail in all levels of the administration and electioneering and party politics would be eliminated. Of course, this argument had a fine moral appeal. As the vast majority of our people are illiterate and ignorant, the burden of the protagonists of this school was "to save them from becoming pawns in the contest for power by political parties and ambitious pressure groups".[3] Jayaprakash Narayan was critical of political parties because he believed that they impeded self-government and the liberation of local initiative. For Narayan, local self-government cannot be created within a system with competing political parties.[4] JP's ultimate idea was "partyless democracy". The All-India Panchayat Parishad (of which JP was chairman) in 1961 went to the extent of advising the States to work for uncontested elections giving rewards to villages electing their panchayat without contest. About 30 per cent of all the panchayat elections at that time were uncontested. The protagonists of Westminster model of parliamentary democracy considered the Sarvodaya's non-political, non-party system as 'visionary'. They even suspected that it would lead to totalitarianism.

The liberal democracy school opposed this concept and wanted political participation. S. K. Dey, for instance, characterised democracy without contest as that of dead people. "A self-sufficient village republic consisting of God-fearing people thinking, believing and acting all alike, is a village dead before it is born. Life cannot spring from such an inanition. Democracy demands ideology and ideals in a perpetual but healthy clash. Only dead people do not compete".[5] In a conference convened at Jaipur in 1964 to discuss the question of panchayati raj and democracy, there was a clash of these two viewpoints. S. C. Jain, Rural Institute Vidya Bhawan, supported the Sarvodaya view while C. P. Bhambri and others argued that the involvement of the parties in the panchayati raj system was both necessary and desirable. The parties would act as tools of modernisation in the villages: "The PR institutions provide a base for progressive parties to operate and fight against the forces of backwardness and tradition. The village people are to be politicised . . . Political parties have to act as a great instrument for the politicisation of the rural masses".[6]

The Santhanam Committee's review of the subject showed that before the advent of Independence and after, there have been proposals for political parties not to contest municipal elections. Occasionally, all parties have stayed from such elections but no resolutions to abstain has been kept for any length of time. During the Nehruvian period till 1964, most political parties abstained from direct participation in elections to panchayats. One reason was that in small wards with 100-500 voters, locally prominent men were likely to succeed. They did not adopt party labels but the political parties used to enroll the elected members to their fold. However, in Tamil Nadu (then Madras) in the panchayat elections in 1964 direct contests were fought between the Congress and the Communists, with 36.3 per cent panchayat members in the State elected unopposed while in Andhra Pradesh the percentage was 45.

The use of party symbols in panchayat elections was not permitted in States except Kerala but even there such symbols were not used at the time of Santhanam Committee review. The Committee was of the opinion that while political party influences cannot be legally banned, it was wrong and unnecessary to encourage their entry into the village by the provision of party symbols. The committee's recommendations merit our attention because it reflected the thinking at that time. The recommendations were:

i. There should be no legal provision prohibiting political parties from influencing panchayati raj elections.
ii. No political party symbol should be issued in any election to panchayati raj institutions.
iii. No representations from political parties should be entertained in relation to panchayati raj institutions.
iv. Official recognition should not be accorded to political party groupings among members of panchayati raj bodies.

Only the first recommendation was at slight variance with the

Sarvodaya stand while all others were in conformity with the JP school. But on the question of unanimity in elections, it took a strong view against the Sarvodaya line, saying "no cash prizes or material inducements or incentives should be offered for unanimity in PR elections". The committee believed that contests were both healthy and educative and recorded having come across villages where anxiety for unanimity and consensus meant continuation of domination by the traditional authorities and the suppression of the new spirit of youth. An experience they had in Gujarat was illuminating.

> "In Gujarat, we visited a village where the panchayat had been unanimously elected for many terms without any change of personnel. When we put the question whether there were no other persons fit to serve in the panchayat and why the same persons were elected continuously for long periods, the only reply was that no one wanted a change".[7]

The conclusion of the Santhanam Committee was important for that time: "Contests are both healthy and educative. Avoidance of contests on a large scale may mean the suppression of youth and it may stunt the growth of Panchayati Raj itself".[8]

We find a remarkable change after about four years of the Santhanam Committee Report. At an important conference on panchayati raj in 1969 at Hyderabad, the majority opinion was for political competitiveness on an ideological basis for both rural and urban India. But the dissenting voice at the meet still believed that the face-to-face community of the Indian village could be better served if it was insulated from political party rivalries.

Soon this theoretical and ideological debate more or less died out. After Nehru's departure from the socio-political scene, the ruling party at the Centre in collusion with the bureaucracy denigrated the panchayati raj institutions, thus throwing out the baby with the bath water. Recalling those days, Govind Narain wrote recently in *Yojana*, "A time came when phoney leaders imposed by the political parties found in this programme a danger to their authority and influence and the word went round that some elections were lost by the ruling party in areas in which the (PR) programme was strong".[9]

The appointment of the Asoka Mehta Committee on December 12, 1977, was a watershed in the history of PRIs. In its report submitted to Prime Minister Morarji Desai on January 21, 1978, it unequivocally said that political parties should be allowed to participate effectively at all levels because it "would make for a clearer orientation towards programmes and would facilitate healthier linkages with higher level political processes. It is also necessary to provide constructive outlet to opposition parties; parties out of power at the State level may be able to chalk out achievement at the district level. Direct elections coupled with programme-based contests would offer greater scope to weaker sections for availing the opportunities offered by the political system".[10]

The first State to put into practice the Asoka Mehta Committee suggestion was West Bengal. After 19 years of inauguration of PRIs in the country, for the first time political parties were officially recognised in the local elections. But the two Congress parties at that time pleaded for non-partisan panchayat polls. The Janata Party was divided on the issue — P.C. Sen strongly opposed party-based contests while Sushil Dhara and Biman Mitra held a different view. The CPI(M) believed that direct involvement of political parties in the working of PRIs would make the panchayat leadership more disciplined and responsible in managing these institutions and would put an end to the age-old tradition of rural coteries reaping the benefits for narrow, sectarian and caste interests. The left parties countered P. C. Sen's 'partyless democracy' thesis with the argument that "partyless candidates could not bring about social change and uphold and strengthen democracy because collective, organised efforts are needed for this; only political parties could bring them about. . . ."[11]

The Karnataka elections to PRIs in 1987 were held officially on party lines. For the first time, individuals who dominated the village scene through their caste, family, money power and bullying tactics, were challenged by candidates put up by national or regional parties. Villages which saw several decades of domination of one particular family or caste had to face stiff challenges. Of course, the rural scene witnessed serious rifts and restlessness even in families because in one family, members were aligned on different party lines. The discussions and debates in tea shops and other public places where elevated to the level of political ideologies, assessment of balance sheet of political parties and tract record of political leaders. The elections proved to be a churning process of ideas and action creating a high level of political awareness.

There is no point in making a fetish about village harmony. As the late Abdul Nazir Sab, then Karnataka's Minister for Panchayati Raj, who worked tirelessly in ushering in a new era of PRIs in the State used to say: "anyway in the villages there is Ramanna-Bhimanna politics. It is a reality. Isn't it healthier that they align on democratic party lines rather than on caste, religion, etc.?[12] The Institute of Social Sciences' study of the working of PRIs in Karnataka since the election has shown that involvement of political parties up to the Zilla Parishad level had generated healthy discussions and debates on definite policies and programmes. Following Karnataka, Andhra Pradesh and Kerala also permitted political parties to participate directly in local elections.

The London County Council from its inception in 1889 has had clearly defined party divisions between its members. Elections are frequently run on party lines. In the local governments in England, political party organisation brings greater coherence and definition into the policies of the governing body. Eric Jackson in his study of local governments in England concluded:

> "Political organisation in local government affairs does have the undoubted advantage, as it does in Parliament, of bringing greater coherence and definition into the policy of the governing body. Where the parties are well organised and disciplined, it is possible to get a decision more quickly than when there is no such organisation. . . . The leader of a political group in power or a representative who can speak with authority on behalf of that group, can be much more sure of his touch when conducting such discussions, and those with whom he is discussing can feel that what he says is more likely to be adopted by the council than when discussions are conducted by a representative who has no such backing".[13]

Of course, one can argue that party discipline will necessarily limit the freedom of its members, that the real power would tend to drift into the hands of the leading politicians and that the party organisation, instead of the elected panchayats may become the real governing body. There are complaints that the CPI(M) in West Bengal, Janata in Karnataka and Telugu Desam Party in Andhra Pradesh have betrayed these tendencies. But this is not a serious problem because of parties and politicians have to endure, they must be sensitive to public criticism. They have to observe the rules of the game.

In our particular social and political situation there may be a tendency for ruling parties to adopt on ostrich-like policy about official contest of parties in local elections. These elections at any point of their tenure will be seen as a verdict on their performance and popularity. More often than not they would like to shy away than face the test. The recently held PR elections in UP without official participation of parties is a case in point. In such contexts, independent candidates of any hue and shade without any internal control or accountability could be in the fray. They claim support of one party or other in a free-for-all situation. It is a well-known fact that the men who attacked the street theatre group led by Safdar Hashmi in UP owed their allegiance to an independent candidate in the local elections. It is an open secret that these independents are not so independent. If a party finds that they have no base, it may support an 'independent'. It was clear to all that the candidate in Hashmi's murder incident was only 'independent' on paper, for it was widely reported that the Congress(I) could not operate in small towns like Ghaziabad and so they put up these so-called 'independents' to spread terror.

Only official party participation will prevent lumpens taking over politics. Therefore, the PRIs and its elections should be seen as nurseries for political leadership. Young blood will be attracted if elections are based on political ideology and inspired by State as well as national political leadership.

Now of course, there is a dearth of political leadership at the lower levels. No wonder that when national parties had to put up candidates at mandal elections in Karnataka, they found it difficult to identify enough party activities. The organic link from Gram Sabha to Lok Sabha can be achieved effectively only through political parties working with the people. Absence of this link has brought about a pathological decay in our democratic system. Wherever official parties have been involved in PRIs, the enthusiasm of local people has been high; the percentage of polling has been unprecedented. For instance it has been established that in the 1978 West Bengal PR elections, one of the most important reasons for widest popular participation was that political parties were officially engaged in the elections. No doubt, this decision (party participation) went a long way in making West Bengal's rural folk very much politically conscious, giving elected panchayat bodies a political standing of their own.[14]

Panchayati raj elections on party basis will certainly heighten politicisation. Almost all parties except Congress(I) welcome politicisation of the people in panchayati raj elections. It seems that the Congress(I) is not favourably disposed towards the politicisation of the masses because it will open the floodgates of demands and assertion of their rights. The ambiguity of Congress(I) is not helpful for genuine devolution of power at the grassroots level.

It is a matter of great significance that in spite of the political problems surfacing at times in the State, the leadership of the National Conference has asserted its faith in panchayat elections on party lines. The National Conference should prove the sceptics wrong.

NOTES

1. *Report of the Committee on Panchayati Raj elections*, Ministry of Community Development and Co-operation, Government of India, New Delhi, 1965, p. 51.
2. K. Subrahmanyam, "Panchayat Reform: A few pitfalls can be avoided", *The Hindusthan Times*, May 18, 1989.
3. Jayaprakash Narayan, *Swaraj for the People*, 1961, see also K. P. Misra, Rajendra Avasthi (eds.), *Politics of Persuasion*, Bombay, 1967.
4. Ibid., p. 51
5. S. K. Dey, *Community Development: A Movement is Born*, Allahabad, 1960, p. 173.
6. Quoted in Mats Kihlberg, *The Panchayati Raj of India*, New Delhi.
7. Santhanam Committee Report, p. 55.
8. Ibid., p. 55.
9. Govind Narain, "Panchayati Raj: Some Reflections", *Yojana*, January 26, 1989, p. 34.
10. *Report of the Committee on Panchayati Raj Institutions*, Ministry of Agriculture and Irrigation, New Delhi, August 1978, p. 52.
11. M. Shiviah, K. B. Srivastava, A. C. Jena, *Panchayati Raj Elections in West Bengal, 1978*, Hyderabad, NIRD, 1980, p. 53.
12. George Mathew, "Panchayat Poll in Karnataka", *The Hindusthan Times*, February 9, 1987.
13. W Eric Jackson, *Local Government in England and Wales*, Penguin Books, 1959, p. 140.
14. A K Mukhopadhyay, *The Panchayat Administration in West Bengal*, Calcutta.

FOUR

Revival of a Democratic Tradition

Mohammad Shafi

DEMOCRACY assumes its basis from the ideal of power from and to the people. Even after 41 years of Independence, we are still striving to achieve the objective of power to the people, having strayed far into the realm of centralisation and concentration of power. Such tendencies have manifested themselves more acutely and intensely on the country's canvas in varied forms. Democratic decentralisation, therefore, has to be pulled out of the crucible of rhetoric and brought on the sound footing of execution and real implementation on the ground. The call of the day is that we must sit up and face the realities and work for strengthening the local institutions as an essential and necessary mechanism for solidifying the roots of democracy in our country and to provide a strong base for social and economic justice in our society.

The concept of democratic decentralisation is in-built and ingrained into the cultural ethos of this country despite the fact that the traditional organisation of politics and structuring of authority was hierarchical. The villages and the village institutions always played a dominant role in our socio-political history and our tradition has been imbued with a unique participatory theme. It is only on account of centralising tendencies that we found that the structures became moribund. The village institutions, instead of being carried and drawn into the mainstream of development, became decrepit organs, creating a chasm in the politico-administrative and economic structuring of society. The revival of the ideological dialogue for the acceleration of democratic decentralisation, finds its emanation in the growing discontentment, a sense of alienation and political distance from the decision-making process.

On the Jammu and Kashmir scenario, the political commitment to the concept of democratic decentralisation is not an innovation or a new idea. It finds prominent place in the manifesto and the policy outline of *Naya Kashmir* as far back as 1944, when Sheikh Mohammad Adbullah while launching it said:

> The All Jammu and Kashmir National Conference considers the "New Kashmir" — programme as a blueprint for the future political and economic setup in the State. We have formulated this programme with this objective in view. From a political angle, it aims at achieving a responsible government based on democratic principles. All institutions of democracy from panchayats to the national assembly will be constituted through due process of election. Independent judicial system shall be an important component of the system and the executive shall be made accountable to the people. *(Translated from Urdu)*

The basic components postulated in the *Naya Kashmir* manifesto were conceived of a purely democratic system with the grassroots level concept of power to the people and from the people. This document can be described as visionary for it gave a system which was based on pure democratic ideals. The main components spelt out in the manifesto reads:

> All the regions of the State shall have equal right to participate in the political power and the same will be decentralised up to the district, block and panchayat levels. The people will elect appropriate institutions so that they can exercise the powers thus transferred to them. Electoral procedure may differ in the case of institutions at different levels. Initially, only such powers and functions will be decentralised which could be easily manageable by these institutions. After they acquire proper experience, the powers and functioning of institutions at the lower level can be made further broad-based. The objective of the system is to strengthen the unity and integrity of the State. *(Translated from Urdu)*

Briefly, the emphasis of our party struggle and its evolution revolved on extinction of the feudal system, restructuring of man-land relationship; to conceive of panchayats and cooperatives as mechanism of dispensation of socio-economic justice and equitable distribution of the benefits of development and doing away with the system of money-lending. Guided by this manifesto, the policies were framed by Sheikh Abdullah during his first term in office as the head of the administration. Further fructification of these ideals came about in the form of *Single Line Administration* during 1975 under his guidance. The model of *Single Line Administration* ushered the process of administrative decentralisation and the building up of participatory base at the district level. This experiment has been able to draw into the vortex of developmental policies and strategies, the representatives of the people. The District Development Boards which are conceived as effective instruments of securing the participatory base with the decentralised planning process, have emerged as effective institutions in our State.

The *Single Line Administration* has ensured the participation of the people in the developmental process and paved the way for decentralisation and delegation of authority. It is unfortunate that due to some political upheavals in the State, these institutions remained dormant for some time. However, with our party having come to power under the dynamic leadership of Dr. Farooq Abdullah, our first step was to revive these institutions to carry on the ideals of decentralisation. Our party's commitment lies in the objective of restoring the democratic character to our local bodies and local institutions. This includes the restoration and revival of panchayati raj institutions. Since we visualise the role of panchayati raj institutions not merely as agencies for accelerating the pace of development but as effective political and democratic institutions, it was therefore, essential for us to pay considerable attention to the structural aspects of these institutions. Our experience with the erstwhile institutions of panchayati raj had not been happy because sans-authority, sans-guidance and sans-delegation of power, these institutions acted more as a source of tension and conflict in the villages and were susceptible to manipulative politics.Radical measures have to be introduced in the structural aspects. It is this particular concern for having effective institutions which has motivated us to conceive of the present Bill introduced in the Legislature.

The new Bill can be described as a radical step because it goes beyond the concept of mere delegation of authority. It encompasses the concept of sharing of power by democratic decentralisation to the grass roots level. We have conceived of three-tier institutions at panchayat halqa, block and district levels. To draw the people's participation in both planning and implementation processes, the full involvement is secured by the process of elections of not only the panch but sarpanchas also. This involvement is also visualised at the block level by introducing the element of direct elections of chairmen of block development councils. This system is a great departure from the earlier conceptual framework and constitutes the greatest strength of the proposed structure. It is being increasingly realised that it is in respect of the local issues that people perceive areas of influence and operationalisation of the decision-making process. Because it is on account of large-scale impact of programmes on the lives of the community that the real operation of any system can be visualised. The more distant the decision-making level, the greater the sense of indifference and alienation. It is by ensuring the involvement of people and effective participation that the roots of democracy can be strengthened, with the people's sense of belonging and identity imbued in the structure. It is only through a participatory base at the grass roots level that democracy can survive and flourish.

Democratic decentralisation is not a hollow process of merely devolving certain powers to the local institutions but a positive and dynamic step which aims at redistribution of power. Unless the profound and fundamental basis of democratic decentralisation in its connotation of power-sharing is realised, these institutions, however well conceived, would not be able to function as effective instruments of politico-administrative development. It is this particular area of redistribution of power and power-equalisation which is the core of the structural pattern we are conceiving.

Participation is a very catchy slogan. As one writer put it, "participation in the decision-making process is like eating spinach — no one is against it in principle because it is good for you". It is this particular trend of only creating institutions in name that we have to be careful about. The local institutions must wield real power and they must be dove-tailed and linked with the total decision-making process, culminating in the institutions at the State level. While formulating our Bill, we have been conscious and aware of many experiments carried out in different parts of the country and of many models like Karnataka, West Bengal and Gujarat, which have been talked about. But our main concern in determining the structural aspects of local institutions has not been guided by any consideration of developing a 'model' or emulating an existing 'model'. The main objective had been to work out a system which can deliver the goods and can fit into the politico-cultural ethos of our State. Our Bill should be seen and perceived in this context and it should not be judged without reference to any particular model.

There are many issues which assail our mind and which have been recurring in the course of discussions generated as a process of introduction of the Bill in the Legislature. Some of the issues raised are:

1. Whether politically our people are prepared for elections at different levels. Some inhibitions and apprehensions have been expressed about this.
2. Whether the system of having direct elections for the sarpanchas and the chairmen of the block development councils would result in tension and conflict within the institutions.
3. What kind of relationship can be evolved between the Chairman of a block development council and the MLA without weakening either's role?
4. To what extent the election process for the different tiers of the institutional framework would allow a positive leadership to emerge from the villages and panchayat halqas? Would it lead to manipulative politics?
5. Whether creation of the block development council would reduce the power and influence of the MLAs?
6. What kind of relationship would emerge between these political institutions and the bureaucracy?
7. What mechanism would be necessary to arm these grassroot level institutions with effective powers and functions both for planning and implementation of programmes?
8. How can the electioneering process be made objective in throwing up leadership and to obviate the use of money power and muscle power?

These are issues which can be debated.

Finally, I would only reiterate that the ultimate success of the decentralised planning process would depend upon the political leadership and a sustained political commitment. Equally important is the concept of a well-motivated bureaucracy to purvey the support in terms of actualisation of this goal. Reorientation and reassessment of perceptions and actions is needed to make the local institutions effective bodies for servicing of developmental needs. We look forward to a thought-provoking and broad-based discussion on various aspects of the Bill and also measures which need to be taken to strengthen the local bodies and the supportive services to make these institutions vibrant organs for accelerating the pace of development of our State.

Democratic politics has proved to be a creative force behind India's historic transformation. We have still to look forward to the process of realising its goals and ideals. This process at times can be frustrating and agonising for it constitutes a race against time itself.

In the words of Jawaharlal Nehru, "We are concerned with the shaping of the future of India. It is, therefore, with a sense of burden of history upon me, upon us, upon this House, that I face this problem".

We rededicate ourselves to this hope, this faith, that we carry the burden of history on us. And with this we march forward.

FIVE

Panchayati Raj in Kashmir: Yesterday, Today and Tomorrow

Riyaz Punjabi

Yesterday

HISTORICALLY, panchayats did exist in India as social institutions and played a meaningful role at intra-socio-cultural levels of rural life. These institutions were not formally structured in the modern sense, but existed as vital and dynamic entities of social life in rural areas. The British advent in India witnessed the emergence of panchayats as statutory bodies with formal structures to play a significant role in the socio-economic development of rural areas. With the statutory recognition of panchayats, some judicial functions were also assigned to them, accorded prestige and authority to them in the system.

In the post-Independence era, great emphasis was laid on revamping and restructuring of panchayats to enable them to play an effective role in the developmental programmes of the state.

As in rest of the country, panchayats existed in Jammu and Kashmir State. They were comprised of the lower level functionaries of the Maharaja, *zaildars, numberdars*, village heads, landlords and other influential people in the rural areas. The function of these panchayats was to settle petty disputes in the villages. A historical evaluation of these institutions and their chequered history reveal how these institutions were manipulated by autocratic rulers and their collaborators for their own ends.

The introduction of local self-government in Jammu and Kashmir State commences with the promulgation of J & K Village Panchayat Regulation No. 1 by the Maharaja of the State in 1935. The preamble of the Act laid down: "Whereas it is expedient to establish in Jammu and Kashmir State the village panchayats to assist in the administration of civil and criminal justice and also to manage the sanitation and other common concerns of the village."

The Act provided for election of panchas, numbering five to seven, of which, one panch would be appointed by the Panchayat Officer or *Wazir-e-Wazarat*. The election would be held on an open stage, with a simple show of hands. The Panchayat Officer was given the discretion to evolve rules for conducting the elections.

In order to form one panchayat, several villages were clubbed together. However, each village was entitled to form one constituency and the larger villages had more than one constituency. The sarpanch of a panchayat had to be elected from among the panchas.

The striking feature of the Act of 1935 was the *provision regarding the right of franchise by the people in the villages and right to be elected as a panch on the panchayat.* The qualifications laid down under the Act for a voter as well as the person seeking election to a panchayat were that the person should be a hereditary State subject, should be living in a rural area, was not insane and was of 21 years old. However, other qualifications, amazingly, were as follows:

i. His revenue tax should be at least five rupees.
ii. He should possess any kind of property valued at Rs 1,000.
iii. His annual income should be at least Rs 700.
iv. He should be at least a matriculate or possess an equivalent academic qualification.

Thus, it is evident that the preponderant majority of people could neither vote nor seek election to any office of a panchayat. It is clear that the panchayati raj institutions envisaged under this Act were meant to be controlled and manned by a small section of the population, a class comprising the rich; in other words those who were the beneficiaries of the autocratic rule of the Maharaja. No common villager had any say in matters related to the panchayats.

The rationale, it appears, was mainly to keep an eye on the activities of National Conference, which was on the vanguard of the struggle for freedom in the State. The autocratic rulers also wanted to use, as is evident from the composition of the panchayats, such bodies to marginalize the influence of the National Conference.

Regarding the functions and powers of the panchayats, their main functions were judicial, that is, to help the government in the administration of civil and criminal justice. Thus, the functions of panchayats at that point of time were predominantly judicial rather than those of local self-government. Ironically, this feature of the panchayati raj system remained quite predominant for a long time to come. It may be mentioned here that out of 58 provisions of the Act, 47 dealt with judicial functions and only 11 dealt with other functions of the panchayat.

One provision, namely Section 61 of the Act, provided for making of arrangements for improving public health, supply of drinking water and the maintenance of village tanks and works of 'public utility'; functions which were never carried out by panchayats.

In connection with the revenue of panchayats, a village fund collected from fees levied for the institution of suits and cases, fines and compensation paid to the panchayats, receipts on account of rates imposed, sums contributed by the royal government and by private persons and sanitation cess, was envisaged.

The panchayats were required to maintain the supervision of government and public property, the supervision of schools, the supervision of the work of village officials and labourers, etc,. and supervision of the construction of public buildings. It is through this provision that the Maharaja's government managed to keep an eye on the activities in the villages.

The raison d'etre of recounting the functions of panchayats in historical perspective is to emphasize the point that they remained disfunctional despite the fact that the functions were well spelt out on the paper. Besides, these bodies were manipulated for purposes other than those of local self-government.

The Panchayat Act of 1935 amended in 1941.

The amended Act of 1941 was an improvement on the earlier legislation. The highlights of this Act were the disqualification of a person to be elected as a panch in case he was a wholetime government servant, or declared an insolvent by a competent court, or if he had been convicted of any offence or subjected to any punishment by a criminal court as would disqualify him in the opinion of the Panchayat Officer from seeking election to a panchayat.

In terms of the amended Act, the valuation of suits to be taken cognizance of by the panchayats was left to the discretion of the parties concerned.

The Act also empowered the panchayats to levy certain taxes and tolls for the benefit of villages.

The Act empowered panchayats to construct, maintain and improve culverts, bridges and public roads, the disposal of drainage water and sewage, the excavation, maintenance and improvement of wells, ponds, springs, and water reservoirs, etc. The cleaning and maintenance of roads, regulating the sites of slaughter houses and examining and inspecting weights and measures was also assigned to panchayats.

The Act transferred all the village public roads, all movable and immovable property to the panchayats along with other structures as the property of the concerned village panchayat.

Elementary and adult education also remained a concern of village panchayats.

The Act further provided for delegation of any power or function except judicial functions, to any of its members and assigned any administrative function to them. A joint committee of various panchayats could undertake more than one matter.

Curiously, most of the functions as mentioned in the foregoing paras remained current in any ongoing legislation on the Panchayati Raj, and yet most of the functions assigned to the panchayats could not be undertaken even in the post-Independence era. The factors responsible for this phenomenon need to be identified.

The responsibilities of establishing panchayats in Jammu and Kashmir were given to the Revenue Department under the Acts of 1935 and 1941. The first panchayats in the Kashmir Valley were established in Srinagar and Baramullah districts, respectively. A Department of Panchayats and Rural Development affiliated to the Revenue Department, was established in 1936. The department was placed under the supervision of a director whose main function was to formulate the general policy for the department and to provide necessary funds to panchayats for the development of their respective areas and supervise their work and functioning.

The Panchayats and Rural Development Department organized 'Dehat-Sudhar Committees' (Village Improvement Committees) to advise panchayats. These committees laid more emphasis on voluntary work (which was called *Halshari* in local parlance) in the villages. The members of this committee included non-panch also or others who were not in any way connected with panchayats or rural development. It is pertinent to point out that these committees were highly misused by the government, even by successive governments in the post-Independence era, to harass and exploit the villagers and ignorant people in rural Kashmir. They had by and large become tools in the hands of undemocratic and repressive ruling regimes.

Today

Land to the tiller, as envisaged in the Naya Kashmir Programme of the National Conference, and implemented soon after Independence, was a watershed in the history of Jammu and Kashmir. This measure, the first of its kind in the sub-continent, was lauded by different sections of society and people belonging to different walks of life in the whole of India. The statutory recognition of proprietary rights on the tillers over the lands tilled by them changed the whole socio-politico and economic landscape of Kashmir. In this backdrop, there was a great opportunity for the panchayati raj system to play its role effectively and meaningfully. The panchayats could oversee the developmental aspect of rural areas through a democratic process at the grassroots level. However, this did not happen. The dismissal of Sheikh Mohammad Abdullah and his ministry and his subsequent arrest changed the whole scenario. The post-1953 era witnessed a continuous phase of undermining democracy and subverting of democratic institutions in the State. Under these circumstances it was futile to expect democracy to function at the grassroots level, namely, the panchayats.

Gradually, the debates, discussions and concern to rejuvenate the panchayati raj system at the national level shook the power elite in Jammu and Kashmir. In a bid to express solidarity with the ruling elite at the Centre, rather than developing any genuine concern for implementing panchayati raj, the State Government passed the Jammu and Kashmir Village Panchayat Act, 1958, "to make better provision for the administration of village panchayats in the Jammu and Kashmir State." This Act repealed the Jammu and Kashmir Village Panchayat Act, Samvat 2008 (corresponding to year 1951).

The historical appraisal of these and other enactments reveal that there has not been much of the difference in the functioning and powers of panchayats. The functions and powers of panchayats under the Act of 1941 (during the Maharaja's regime) and under the Act of 1958 have, by and large, remained the same. However, the tactics of manipulating panchayats changed with the circumstances. During the autocratic rule of the Maharaja, the panchayats were manipulated by laying down 'special qualifications' for the voters as well as officers to be elected to run the panchayats. Under the Panchayati Raj Act of 1958, any 'panch', 'sarpanch' or 'naib-sarpanch' could be removed from office in case his conduct in office was 'undesirable' or "his removal (was) desirable in *the interest of the public.*"

Under this Act the 'prescribed authority' would fix the number of panchas from time to time which would not be less than seven and not more than 11 members. The 'prescribed authority' would also determine the 'number of panches to be elected and number of panchas to be nominated from time to time.' The manner or number of elections and nominations, respectively, was not provided under the Act.

Interestingly before Independence, the Maharaja's regime provided sufficient assistance to panchayats in Jammu and Kashmir. In 1937-38, when the Panchayats were established for the first time in the State, the government provided an assistance of Rs. 40,000 to such bodies. This assistance rose to Rs. 3,85,000 in the year 1945-49. This was in addition to the resources mobilised internally by panchayats. Ironically, the State government has not been providing any assistance to panchayats even though both the enactments, those of 1951 and 1958, made a provision to this effect. The Act of 1958 laid stress on revenue resources through taxes without any commitment on the part of the government in this behalf.

The panchayats in the State continued to remain dormant even after the Indira Gandhi-Sheikh Abdullah Accord of 1975.

The popular government in 1977 introduced the *Single Line Administration* with the objective of securing a mechanism for developing the planning process at the district level and to take complete account of resource endowment. This administration also initiated a process of equitable development of various areas within a district. However, in spite of these well-meaning administrative measures, the panchayats could not be re-invigorated and remained without any linkages to other institutional framework.

It is in this back-drop of panchayati raj in the State that the Jammu and Kashmir Panchayati Raj Act, 1989, appeared on the socio-political scenario, raising new hopes for the participation of people in the economic and democratic process at the grassroots level. It is, therefore, desirable to closely examine some important provisions of the Act.

Tomorrow

The Jammu and Kashmir Panchayati Raj Act, 1989, aims at introducing the panchayati raj system in a very effective way in the State of Jammu and Kashmir. The Act, according to the preamble, proposes that the State usher in a second era of socio-political revolution; the first one being the agrarian reforms of 1947, which gave land to the tiller.

The Act envisages avenues of people's participation in the decision-making and decision-implementing processes. It proposes to involve the common people in policy planning and thereby ensuring their participation in the socio-political process at the grassroots level. It appears that the framers of the Act, having kept the earlier experiments of various States in India in view, ensured to avoid pitfalls which made the panchayati raj system dysfunctional in most of the States in post-Independence India.

The rationale of the Act, as provided in the statement of objective, is "to promote and develop panchayati raj in the State as an instrument of vigorous local self-government to secure the effective participation of the people in the implementation of development programmes". The Act provides for the establishment and constitution of the following authorities:

1. Halqa panchayats;
2. Block Development Councils;
3. District Planning and Development Boards; and
4. Panchayat Adalats.

The Act gives wide ranging powers to the halqa panchayat, which is the soul of the system. It is the centre around which the planning, developmental and political activities of the people at the grassroots level would revolve. In order to ensure the people's participation in planning, the Act provides that the halqa panchayat be *under a legal duty* to prepare plans for the development of the area and undertake measures for the implementation of the development plans. The halqa panchayat is required to deal with the problems of soil conservation, water management, social forestry, rural industrialisation, various aspects of agriculture, animal husbandry and sanitation and health. The halqa panchayat is further required to frame regulations relating to construction of buildings, shops and entertainment houses, to check offensi. , and dangerous trades, maintain the ecological balance and to protect the environment. The halqa panchayats are also required to formulate regulations for consumer protection and for evolving the plans for removing poverty and creating avenues of employment through new programmes.

The panchayats shall be involved in the implementation of schemes of universalization of elementary education.

The halqa panchayat shall have a fund which shall be called the Halqa Panchayat Fund. This fund will be raised from the grants of the government, loans granted by the financial institutions, or other such agencies, taxes and duties, rates and fees levied by or under the Act. All these revenues would be diverted towards the Halqa Panchayat Fund. However, the Act does not specifically make a provision about allocation of loans from governmental and other financial institutions for developmental purposes. The absence of these facilities would hamper, a great deal, the developmental work of panchayats.

New Power Structure

The Bill thus appears to envisage the creation of a new power structure with its roots among the people at the grassroots level. It is, in fact, an entirely new experiment in the socio-political system of the State.

The creation of a new authority of an elected sarpanch in a particular area will be a new political development in the State. It may be pointed out here that a sarpanch is not an *alta idem* to another political authority, i.e., MLA (Member of Legislative Assembly), but there is definite scope for building tension between the two, i.e., an elected 'sarpanch' and an 'MLA'. It would be a litmus test for the government to see that the sarpanch of a halqa exercises his functions and powers without the interference of an MLA. Moreover, an MLA is to bear in mind that in view of ever-increasing governmental activities and expanding horizons of people's aspirations, it is not possible for him/her to be in a position to accomplish the gigantic task of economic development in a particular area. Hence he/she should adjust to the changing environment and welcome the new structure which will share his/her responsibilities.

The decentralisation of power at the top level would lead to the decentralisation of power at every level. This includes decentralisation of political power and administrative and bureaucratic authority. In the absence of a culture of decentralisation of power and authority, particularly in Jammu and Kashmir, the Act may generate tensions at various levels of the political and administrative structure of the government. The government has to devise means to contain these tensions.

Remote Control

The Panchayati Raj Act makes it obligatory on the part of halqa panchayat to develop an area, and it is obligatory upon all the halqa panchayats to implement the development plans of the area. A halqa panchayat under the Act can be superceded in case government is of the opinion that it is incompetent or persistently defaults in the performance of duties imposed on it under the Act. However, where a particular halqa panchayat is not favourably inclined towards the government, or does not fall in line with the ruling party, it may face the consequences by way of squeezing of funds and throttling of resource channels by the government. Thus the government may in a subtle manner decrease the grants and bring the halqa panchayat to a point of non-performance and consequently supercede it.

The Act provides that a halqa panchayat shall comprise of seven members including the sarpanch. However, the Act provides that the competent authority, i.e., the government, may nominate two members in case it is of the opinion that women or Scheduled Caste/any other class are not represented in the halqa panchayat. Thus, the government proposes to arrogate the powers to nominate two members in a halqa panchayat of seven members. The term "any other class" not being an *ejesdum generis* to the provision mentioned gives wide powers to the government to nominate two persons of its choice. Thus, it is very easy for the ruling party to select two members to gain the majority control over the halqa panchayat. This would also result in pressurising the Sarpanch to toe the line and would, consequently, affect the autonomous character of the halqa panchayat adversely.

Pertinently, the Balwant Rai Mehta Committee recommendation, which was accepted by the National Development Council in 1959 and later reproduced by the Administrative Reforms Commission Report, 1969, provides that "the Panchayati Raj Institutions need not submit their budgets for approval to higher authorities if they frame their budgets including expenses within their resources, namely, revenues expected to be raised and the grants promised to them, the obligatory expenses taking precedence over the optional. If they budget for an expenditure in excess to such resources, the budgets should be approved by the authority which is in a position to meet the excess, namely, the zila parishad or the government, as the case may be".

It is worthwhile to consider the proposal of separation of funds to halqa panchayats into two channels, one by their own resources and the second comprising funds allocated by the government to them. It appears reasonable to allow the halqa panchayat to spend the funds raised by them on their own within the guidelines laid down by the Council or Board.

Block Development Council

The Act envisages constitution of a Block Development Council for every block in the State.

The Block Development Council shall have the functions of construction, maintenance and supervision of inter-halqa panchayat communication systems. The council shall provide administrative and technical guidance to the halqa panchayat and shall review its work. Among other notable functions, the council shall undertake measures for effective supervision and monitoring of various developmental programmes which have been undertaken by halqa panchayats.

The Act proposes to constitute a Block Development Council Fund comprising grants made by the government on per capita basis and revenue assigned by the District Development and Planning Board.

A Continuum of Power

The establishment and constitution of the Block Development Council is a continuum of the efforts to create a new power structure under the Panchayati Raj Act. The remarkable feature of the council is the direct election of the chairman and exclusion of members of Legislature and Parliament from holding any office in it.

The powers and functions as mentioned under the Act pertaining to the council are, however, quite vague. It would have been appropriate to make the council responsible for undertaking measures for effective supervision and monitoring of various developmental programmes which the panchayats would undertake and the Act provides for that. Similarly, assigning the job of formulating and implementing the plans relating to agriculture, rural development, etc., appear to be duplication of the functions and efforts of halqa panchayats which have to formulate and implement plans in these areas.

The District Planning and Development Board

The Panchayati Raj Act envisages the constitution of District Planning and Development Boards.

The Chief Minister of the State has been empowered to nominate a minister to be the chairman of the District Planning and Development Board.

Functions and Powers of District Planning Board

The District Planning and Development Board would be the highest authority in the power structure of the proposed panchayati raj system. The Act provides that all the funds granted by the government or any other agency meant for the development of the district will flow through the District Planning and Development Board as per the district plans. The Board shall have the power to consider and guide the formulation of development programmes for the district and undertake priorities for various schemes to consider issues relating to the speedy development and economic upliftment of the district. Among other functions, the Board shall formulate and finalise the plan and non-plan budget, lay down the policy guidelines for the Block Development Council and halqa panchayats, supervise and coordinate poverty alleviation and employment generation programmes and extend assistance to halqa panchayats in this behalf.

Real Fountainhead

Whereas the Act proposes to create a new power structure with its two tiers having roots among the people, the Act proposes to establish the third tier at the apex of the new power structure with the overwhelming majority of government officials and politicians, who otherwise did not find place in the halqa panchayats or Block Development Councils. Thus, it appears that where, on the one hand an attempt has been made to decentralise the power, on the other, the real fountainhead remains where it was. In practical terms, the District Planning and Development Boards have been empowered to "guide" the formulation of developmental plans for the districts, which means the programmes will virtually be formulated by such Boards and that the priorities remain in their hands. A point to be noted is that in case the planning and development programme are "guided" and "considered" by the District Planning and Development Board, the same Board has to finalise the plan and non-plan budget, approve the budget of the Block Development Council and is to be the funding agency. Being dominated by government officials and politicians, is it not clear as to who will wield power in the new structure? It may be pointed out here that the Balwantrai Mehta Committee, observing the powers to be enjoyed by the Collector, observed that "the Collector should have power to obtain information regarding the working of those institutions so that he may be able to give timely and proper advice necessary in the public interest". "However", the committee maintained, "it should be clearly understood that the advisory role does not empower him to exercise supervisory and controlling authority over the working of Panchayati Raj Institutions". The recommendation may be considered for the survival of the system.

Conclusion

Kashmir has witnessed fluctuating fortune with regard to the democratic process as well as democratic functioning of the institutions in the post-Independence period. The panchayati raj system might have suffered setbacks in other States of India as well, but in the Kashmir context it has entirely different connotations and dimensions. In case policy planners are convinced that people in Kashmir should be actively involved in the democratic process and be made a vibrant party to the process of participatory democracy, panchayati raj offers an opportunity as well as challenge to them.

The brief appraisal of panchayati raj legislations and functioning of this system effectively brings forth the stark realisation that this system was manipulated concurrently in case of Kashmir. Thus, the present Act has raised the expectations of reviving the system and providing the people an opportunity to participate in the developmental activities through democratic processes. Therefore, the policy planners should ensure that the potential of manipulation under the present legislation should be eliminated. A stage has come where the human being as a focal point of all the activities need to be recognised. Therefore, the political structure has to evolve a mechanism to bring about the human welfare through human efforts and needs to be oriented to their capacities and capabilities. Thus, the mechanisms of manipulative politicising, through the provisions of law, need to be done away with. The present legislation on panchayati raj in Kashmir provides such a mechanism and there is a need to eliminate this and lessen the range of remote control operation. S.K. Dey, the doyen of panchayati raj system in India, aptly remarked that if a man from a village can become a minister or a prime minister, why can't he run (from planning to execution level) the affairs of his panchayat. If we are sincere in our intentions to have rural self-government, we have to trust the capabilities of the rural people.

It is ironical that a State and its leadership which adopted such a revolutionary measure of 'Land to the tiller' should have missed incorporating a provision of compulsory minimum wages to labourers through panchayats. In the same manner, as historical appraisal reveals, elections to panchayats and even dissolution of panchayats have taken place at the discretion of ruling elites. Amazingly, the latest legislation on the subject is again silent in this matter. In case the faith of people in the State of Jammu and Kashmir in the democratic process is to be re-affirmed, the provision of compulsory elections to panchayats is a *sine qua non*.

SIX

A Flawed Legislation

Balraj Puri

THE Jammu and Kashmir Panchayati Raj Bill was passed by both the houses of the State Legislature barely a month and a half before the Prime Minister of India introduced the Constitution (64th Amendment) Bill in Parliament on May 15, 1989, on the same subject.

This latter Bill authorises the State legislatures to enact laws about the panchayati raj institutions while giving constitutional sanctions to their powers and functions. Even after the passage of the Central Bill, the States need to pass their own laws. As on account of Article 370 of the Constitution, the Central Bill does not apply to the State of Jammu and Kashmir, it had in any case to pass its own law without having to conform to the new constitutional provisions on panchayati raj.

Moreover, the peculiar multi-ethnic, multi-linguist and multi-religious character of the State necessitated variation from the uniform panchayati raj pattern being proposed for the rest of the country. The thrust of the case for panchayati raj elsewhere, for instance, is on devolution of power and providing a sense of participation of the people, in Jammu and Kashmir State, it has all along also been conceived as an instrument of accommodating its wider diversities.

How far does the law of the State meet its peculiar needs and how does it compare with the proposed national pattern in its devolutionary content?

References to the panchayati raj system are found in the policy statements of the political parties and leaders of the freedom movement in Jammu as well as in Kashmir. It, for instance, finds prominent mention in the *New Kashmir*, the political manifesto adopted in 1944 by the National Conference, which spearheaded the freedom movement in the Kashmir Valley. Article 45 of the document defines people's panchayat as organs of the State power in districts, tehsils and villages. Its activities cover "Maintenance of State order, observance of laws and the protection of the rights of citizens, local economic and cultural development and civil defence".

As the National Conference was essentially a movement of regional nationalism of Kashmir Valley for which it demanded the right of self-determination, separate from the rest of the State, its manifesto did not adequately deal with inter-regional problems. But after Sheikh Abdullah's return to power in 1975, following his accord with the Government of India, the need was felt to take cognizance of the existing realities and redraft the manifesto accordingly. The task was assigned to this writer whose draft was unanimously adopted by the National Conference in 1976. It declares: "In order to respect regional personalities and accommodate their respective needs and sentiments, the party . . . proposes to reorganise the internal constitutional setup of the State which would provide regional autonomy and further decentralise political power through appropriate institutional arrangements at the district, block and village levels".

It is obvious that this concept of decentralisation was directly related to its integrating role and covered all levels from region to village. For devolution of power at various levels alone could give assurance and a sense of belonging to various ethnic and religious communities in a State which has a unique chain of wheels within wheels — a Muslim majority State within a Hindu majority country, a Hindu majority region within a Muslim majority State, Muslim majority districts within Hindu majority region, Hindu majority blocks within Muslim majority districts and Muslim majority villages within Hindu majority blocks.

In recognition of these realities, the Jammu and Kashmir State People's Convention, convened and presided over by Sheikh Abdullah and attended by almost the entire political spectrum of the Kashmir Valley, unanimously adopted, on 8 October 1969, a five-tier constitutional setup for the State, which aimed at "widest possible decentralisation of power at regional, district, block and panchayat levels, without jeopardising the integrity of the State."

On the eve of his return to power, Abdullah sought cooperation of the representatives of Jammu and Ladakh at a convention in Srinagar in August 1974 on the basis of the decentralised polity adopted at the People's Convention. When he became Chief Minister of the State in February 1975, he repeatedly declared his intention to appoint a commission of experts to work out details of the five-tier constitution. Somehow, he never implemented his declarations.

One of the first announcements of his son, Dr Farooq Abdullah, after resumption of power in November 1986 was to appoint a five-member commission headed by this author to implement the assurance of his father. The terms of reference of the proposed commission, as conveyed to me as its chairman-designate, were:

> With a view to strengthening the unity of the State and its secular basis, improving interregional relations, ensuring sense of participation and equitable share in power and development to all sections of the people, the commission is required to make recommendations for:
>
> 1. appropriate measure of regional autonomy and further devolution of power to lowest unit of administration; and
> 2. any other measures to remove tensions and irritations between the regions.

While Dr. Farooq Abdullah, too, eventually wriggled out of his commitment to appoint the commission, it is clear that the entire debate on decentralisation of power in Jammu and Kashmir kept its integrating role in focus and gave equal importance to all the four tiers within the State. The focus of the debate on panchayati raj in the rest of the country has mainly been on its democratising role but there too, it has been regarded as a federal continuum, part of the process of transfer of power from Centre to States and lower tiers.

The terms used since the Balwant Rai Committee recommended it in 1959, signifies much more than the system of village panchayats which was traditionally in vogue in India. It is a logical extension of the federal system of the Centre-State relations, under the Constitution, to units within the State.

Judged by this criterion, the Jammu and Kashmir Panchayati Raj Act of 1989 does not satisfy the spirit of the philosophy of the panchayati raj. For contrary to all declarations of Sheikh Abdullah, his son Farooq Abdullah and their party, National Conference, the regional tier is conspicuous by its absence in the new law.

Just as leaders of many States have expressed apprehensions that the Central law on panchayati raj might erode the identity of the State and thus undermine the principle of federalism, similarly, people in the regions, particularly in Jammu and Ladakh, can genuinely fear that the panchayati raj law of the State might undermine their regional identity and thus lead to centralisation of power. As in a State like Jammu and Kashmir, regional identities are the main cementing force among various communities, their erosion would automatically force communal alignments on the people and weaken the secular basis of the State.

The Jammu and Kashmir Panchayati Raj enactment thus does not serve the interest of integration as the concept was supposed to do. As far as its devolutionary role is concerned, it would also be found wanting as compared to the pattern of the panchayati raj envisaged in the Constitution (64th Amendment) Bill.

In giving prominence to the district, the State law would seem to conform to the proposed national law. In fact, constitution of the statutory district planning and development board, as a part of the panchayati raj, is an innovation in the State. Eventhough the district boards exist in the State, they have no statutory authority. The previous law, Village Panchayat Act of 1958 (which was last amended in 1973) merely provided for two tiers i.e., village and block. However, while the Constitution (64th Amendment) Bill in Parliament provides for direct elections to panchayati raj institutions at all levels, not a single member of the district board, under the State law, shall be directly elected. Its chairman shall be nominated by the government. Other members include chairmen of the block development councils, town area committees and municipal councils in the districts. MLAs and MPs would be ex-officio members of the District Board. Though they are elected, it is well known that voters often choose different parties at local, State and national levels as the issues are different at these levels. Members of the Assembly and Parliament, in their capacity as members of the district boards, cannot therefore be said to represent the wishes of the people. In many States where MLAs and MPs are members of the district boards, they have no voting rights. But under the Jammu and Kashmir law, they shall have these rights also.

Further, the executive authority of the district boards, in the State law, entirely rests with the government officers. For according to the law, the district development commissioner, shall be the chief executive of the district board and shall be assisted by the district level heads of department in dischrge of his functions.

At the block level also, unlike the Central Bill, the State law does not provide for direct election of any member. It shall comprise of sarpanchas of halqa panchayats and chairman of the marketing society within the jurisdiction of the block. The provision for election of the chairman of the block council by an electoral college of sarpanchas and panchas of the panchayats in that block was added at the final stage of passage of the Bill in the Assembly. The original draft had provided, like the Central Bill, for direct election of the office-bearers of the block development council. The draft which had provided for a directly elected secretary, was further modified in the Assembly to make the block development officer an ex-officio secretary; thus bringing the block development council also under the influence of the government. The government shall also have power, under the law to nominate two members to give representation to women, scheduled caste or any other class. The Central Bill provides for 33 per cent reservation for women and, according to the population ratio, for the scheduled castes but it does not provide for any nomination at any level. The State law provides for nomination but not reservation. Further, the term 'other class' is so vague that it can be used by the State government to nominate any person on the block council to represent it.

It is only at the halqa panchayat level where all members shall be directly elected. But even at this level, a government employee as the village level worker, shall be the member secretary who shall thus ensure the presence of government at the base of the panchayati raj system. Moreover, the government shall have the power to nominate two members on the halqa panchayat on the same pattern as it does on the block council. There shall be no reservation for women and scheduled castes. Their representatives shall be nominated by the State government in as arbitrary manner as it may like.

One more flaw in the State law with regard to the functions of the halqa panchayat is that its members have not been made accountable to the people after they are elected. There is no provision for a gram sabha which could act as a sort of assembly for the panchayat and could meet once or twice a year to pass the budget and exercise some control on the working of the panchayat; including the right to pass a vote of no-confidence in it or any of its members and elect new members in their place.

In Karnataka, for instance, the gram sabha is the lowest tier of the panchayati raj, comprising all voters of the zilla parishad in a village. It meets at least twice a year to discuss implementation of development programmes, proposals for new programmes for development, building up of a land army, programme of education and other matters.

The Central Council of Local Self-government, meeting at Hyderabad in 1959, had observed that where legislation has provided for gram sabha and panchayat, it has to report the progress and present the budget. "This has the beneficial effect of getting social sanction behind panchayat activities and makes for greater people's participation", the Council felt.

In June 1962, the Union Ministry of Community Development, by a resolution held: "the objective of panchayati raj is to establish a participating democracy so that at the village level, the gram sabha, consisting of all adult residents of the village, should not only deliberate upon but also participate with its executive, namely the gram panchayat, in planning and implementing the various programmes".

A study team appointed by the Government of India in August 1962, also reported: "the gram sabha could alone help to create a climate which would secure the essentials of democracy and endow the total governmental structure of the village community with a social base".

Evidently the law-makers of Jammu and Kashmir did not think it advisable to provide the panchayati raj with a social base, social sanction and direct popular participation as reports of many expert committees and common use would suggest.

This issue of supersession of the panchayati raj institutions has been agitating panchayati raj votaries for a long time. One of the major objectives of the 64th amendment to the Constitution, according to the Prime Minister, is to prevent "Sickness of unending suspensions and dissolutions" of the panchayati raj institutions. Jammu and Kashmir State law empowers the government to supercede panchayats for incompetence or default subject to two conditions: (a) show cause notice shall be served and (b) period of supersession shall not exceed six months.

The repeated Act of 1958 also provided for show cause notice and a provision that "the government may any time within six months establish another panchayat in place of the superseded or the dissolved panchayat." But this did not prevent the government from not holding fresh elections to the panchayats till 1989 which were dissolved in 1984.

Perhaps the use of the word 'shall' instead of 'may' in the present law might make a difference. But unlike the Central Bill, the State law has not made a corresponding amendment in its constitution to make it constitutionally mandatory for fresh elections of the panchayats within six months.

Further, as provision for supersession of the panchayats by the State governments is analogous to the power of the Union Government to dismiss the State governments under Article 356 of the Constitution, it should have been obligatory on the part of the State government to submit any act of supersession of a panchayat to the State Assembly for its approval in the manner in which the Union Government is required, under the Constitution, to seek approval of Parliament of any action taken by it under Article 356; so that if the power of supersession is misused, members of the Assembly get an opportunity to expose and criticise it.

A prerequisite of the success of the panchayati raj system is its financial viability and autonomy. The Karnataka law on the subject, for instance, allocates Rs. 10 per person per year residing in the area of the mandal panchayat. Out of this 25 per cent shall be paid by the government to the zilla parishad. Another important feature of the Karnataka Act is the provision of the Finance Commission for the zilla parishads to be set up by the government which would ensure objective allocation of resources. The 64th Amendment also provides for appointment of a Finance Commission by the State governments to make recommendations for (a) determination of the taxes, duties, tolls and fees which may be assigned to panchayats, (b) distribution between the State and panchayats of the net proceeds of taxes, duties etc. and (c) grant-in-aid to the panchayats by the States.

In Uttar Pradesh, panchayats have an assured source of income in allocation of land revenue to them.

The Jammu and Kashmir law neither fixes minimum amount of grants-in-aid by the State to the panchayats nor provides for any autonomous machinery for objective allocation of funds. It has no assured source of income either. The law, therefore, does not ensure financial viability and autonomy of the panchayats and leaves enough financial power in the hands of the State government which it could use arbitrarily to influence the working of the panchayats.

Panchayati adalat is another important feature of the new panchayati raj law of the State. For, the modern system of justice is not only very expensive and time-consuming but it also virtually inaccessible to the vast majority of the people in rural and far off areas. Panchayati adalats have been used in many States to supplement the formal judicial system by reviving and legitimising the traditional system of justice.

The provision for panchayati adalat in the Jammu and Kashmir law should, therefore, be welcomed. One would, however, like its scope to be widened to include subjects like untouchability, pollution and other crimes against the community. But it is equally important to protect freedom of conscience and right of dissent of individuals against community prejudices and superstitions.

However, by empowering the State government to nominate members of the panchayati adalat and to remove its chairman or any member, the new law robs independence of the institution of justice at the grassroots level. It amounts to supplementing the judicial system and the traditional system of justice, both supposed to be independent of the executive, by a third sector of justice controlled by the State government.

There may be cases of misconduct by chairmen or members of the panchayati adalats which may require their removal. But the power to take action against them should be entrusted to an appropriate judicial authority so that the panchayati adalats become an informal extension of the judicial system and remain immune from bureaucratic influences. Similarly, the authority to appoint members of the panchayati adalat should also not vest with the government. Either the halqa panchayat or a judicial body should have the power to do so.

The new State law has raised a controversy by depriving displaced persons who migrated from Pakistan in 1947 to Jammu and have since settled there of the right to vote in panchayats to which they were entitled under the Act of 1958. The ruling alliance might hope to get some political mileage in Kashmir by their disfranchisement. But as the number of such displaced persons is an insignificant part of the total electorate, their limited participation in self-government at local level in a block or two cannot have any impact on State politics. The State could, therefore, afford to take a humanitarian view of the matter and retain the elementary right of these persons.

The Jammu and Kashmir Panchayati Raj Act does not accept the jurisdiction of the Union Election Commission "for superintendence, direction and control of the conduct of elections in the State" nor that of the Comptroller and Auditor-General of India (CAG) "for the audit of accounts of the panchayats" as the 64th Amendment to the Constitution proposes to do for other States of the country.

The autonomy of the panchayati raj system in Jammu and Kashmir from federal institutions like the Election Commission and CAG may not be an unmixed gain, in view of not-so-proud record of either fair elections or of an incorruptible administration of the State. Moreover, the law of the State not only falls considerably short of the measure of devolution that is proposed under the 64th Amendment for the rest of the country, but the process of devolution is matched by extension of the bureaucratic authority at every level.

Whatever be the case of the opposition against a Central initiative for the panchayati raj legislation, the Jammu and Kashmir Government of which the Congress party is a coalition partner, has used its independent legislation, to which it is entitled under Article 370 of the Constitution, to circumvent constitutional provisions that would restrict bureaucratic control over the panchayati raj institutions elsewhere.

The State is not only independent of the federal institutions like the Election Commission and CAG, it has also not amended its own constitution corresponding to the 64th Amendment in the Indian Constitution. Such an amendment would not have compromised autonomy of the State but would have protected the interests of the panchayati raj institutions against bureaucratic encroachments by, say, making reelection of superseded panchayats constitutionally mandatory and reserving a list of subjects in the constitution for exclusive management by the panchayats.

Lack of trust in the people seems to be the only plausible explanation for the type of law the State has passed. Without trying to read motives into the intentions of the ruling parties, the distrust could possibly be attributed to the fact that the people of a sensitive border State are supposed to be more susceptible to communal and secessionist appeals from across the border. Further, it may be argued that recognition of regional identities might threaten the unity of the State.

The second argument is directed against the identity and

autonomy of the States within India and its federal constitution. Enough empirical evidence supplements theoretical arguments to conclusively prove that federalism ensures unity better than a unitary system in non-homogeneous societies. A unitary constitution in a diverse State like Jammu and Kashmir within a federal country, is, in any case an anomalous situation and generates most of the tensions and problems in one of the most crucial States of the Indian Republic.

As far as the first argument is concerned, distrust of the people and regimentation of the system are not the best means to wean them away from communal and secessionist propaganda. Distrust, in any case, begets distrust. However, while decentralisation is an essential measure to promote democratisation and integration, it is not a sufficient condition for the growth of these principles.

In a system that lacks other democratic prerequisites such as democratic temper of the leaders and the people and one which lacks other democratic institutions like a balanced and healthy party system, independent judiciary, free press and neutral and competent administration, grievance redressal machinery, fair and free elections and an egalitarian economy, mere decentralisation of institutions, sans power, would only sharpen instruments of regimentation and tyranny.

Likewise, a society that is riven with ethnic and communal tensions would hardly be able to get full advantage of the integrating role of decentralisation and federalism and would be tempted to seek stability in further centralisation.

Whether lack of decentralisation is responsible for the decline of democracy and rise of communal and regional tensions in Jammu and Kashmir or undemocratic trends and tensions are the outcome of a unitary constitution imposed on a vastly heterogeneous State and concentration of power — are issues of wider debate. But where else could one make a beginning to break the vicious circle, where cause is the effect and effect is also the cause, except by innovating institutional reforms and trusting the people by giving them a genuine sense of involvement and participation? That would require a conceptually different approach than that of the present State law on panchayati raj, adoption of a federal constitution for the State, withdrawal of some authority of the State government from institutions of panchayati raj and a measure of self-denial on the part of the ruling political leadership.

SEVEN

Does the Bill Give Power to the People?

Sushma Choudhary

THE country's landscape of public administration is gripped by the slogan of "power to the people", described as "people's participation" in the decision-making process. This concept encompasses the entire socio-political and economic structure. More recently, we have countenanced a tremendous pressure being exerted by intellectuals, thinkers and practitioners of public administration for pulling the theme of people's participation out of the crucible of conceptual framework and debate and to be physically installed on the firmament of the democratic process for stability and concrete realisation. The assiduous recurrence of the sense of urgency for evolving and devising suitable structures and strategies for actualisation of the goal of people's participation emanates from the increasing sense of powerlessness and alienation from the power structure and hugeness of the labyrinthine institutional framework as perceived at the people's end. The ostensible manifestation of the undercurrent of distress is evinced in the bourgeoning feeling of disillusionment, which at times has taken the veneer of an agitational attitude, subversive activities and scant regard for systems and values.

Concomitant to this is a growing realisation that there is more to development than the mere pursuit for growth:

- Economic growth alone has not assured an egalitarian system or equitable distribution of development.
- Economic growth by itself has failed to promote the well-being of the community, to remove poverty or even to narrow

down the gap between the rich and the poor.

— Development, with its main focus on the growth syndrome, has rather accentuated the hiatus between the rich and the poor by rendering the systems subservient to the exploitative powers.

The development concept, therefore, has more to its definitional aspect rather than a mere process for achieving economic growth. The present day slogan dinned continuously is that growth has to be tempered with the concept of equity and social justice. The determinant factors for a sound developmental structure are the improvement of the quality of life and growth of the personality. Development has come to be regarded as a process by which the individual is enabled 'to live' and to 'live to have'. In this contextual background, harnessing of people's participation has become a key factor for stimulating the developmental process. It is this maelstrom of development which has placed the focus on 'democratic decentralisation' and 'public participation' as the key elements in the strategy aimed at the development and well-being of the country. It is unfortunate that the concept of 'popular participation' is not amenable to any specific definition. That is why the concept of public participation is involved in the welter of thought processes and mere rhetoric. One has to look beyond the discussion and diagnostic analysis what public participation means and implies. Some of the aspects governing the conceptual framework of public participation are as follows:

1. The outlook on the area of public participation remains a mystery due to seemingly discordant streams of thought governing the framework of democracy from which it derives its legitimacy. At one end of the spectrum are those who view democracy as a means to realisation of human potentialities. At the other end are those who conceive of democracy from the standpoint of viability with the value of efficiency, coherence and innovation.
2. Another critical dimension governing the public administration concept is that of the increased requirement of specialisation owing to the growth in complicity and size of the organisations. The plea is that given the scale and scope of organisational expanse, the greater is the need for specialisation, centralised control and delimitation of tasks.

Modern technology, it is pleaded, calls for a process of specialisation and so the concept of public participation is difficult to aspire for.

3. Another dimension is the demand for stability of the political system. Many thinkers have alluded to the dangers inherent in the increase in participation, particularly on the part of the ordinary man. It is pointed out by those opposed to the concept of popular participation, that the masses are incompetent and at best pliable, inert stuff or at worst aroused and unruly creatures possessing an insatiable proclivity to undermine culture and liberty. Their involvement and participation would undermine the stability of the system, it is argued.
4. Equally forceful is the plea putforth by the rationalists who emphasise the quality of the decisions rather than the process for decision-making. Their argument is that it is not relevant who governs or who makes decisions but what decisions are made and how a system is administered. This can be couched in the efficiency syndrome.

From the assorted viewpoints which have been narrated above, one aspect which looms large on the canvas of any debate concerning the realisation of democratic decentralisation of participatory base, relates to faith in the common man. The reconstruction of any story of democratic decentralisation unfolds the commitment and faith in the common man to govern himself and to participate in the decision-making process. Once there is a recognition and reckoning of the importance of man in the whole process, the institutional framework which is devised for the purpose of actualisation of the goal of participatory administration or political structure would be viewed only as a mechanism rather than an end. Therefore, the evolution process seeking for institutional basis for ensuring the participation of the people in the developmental process stems from the deep-rooted commitment or recognition of the man and his potentiality. However, sound the institutional base may be or the structural aspects may be conceived rationally but these would appear to be hollow unless and until there is a conscious effort to restore the common man at the centre of the system. It is from the standpoint of resurrection of faith in the capability of the common man to decide for himself and others that the efficacy and feasibility of any institutional arrangement can be viewed, gauged and evaluated.

Given the backdrop of the conceptual aspects as well as the practical dimensions of the concept of people's participation in the decision-making process, the perspective of the evolution of the concept of panchayati raj system in Jammu and Kashmir is proposed to be examined. The panchayats as the local institutions of self-government are lying moribund for a very long time specially from 1982. Prior to this, the panchayati institutions existed only at the grassroots level and there was no linkage with any other institutional framework at the block or the district level. Apart from the panchayats there were panchayat adalats also constituted in Jammu and Kashmir as an important instrument for dealing with local issues and legal aspects. The role and significance of the local institutions emerged as a potent and predominant factor with the launching of an experimentation for decentralisation of the planning process at the district level under the scheme known as *Single Line Administration*. Jammu and Kashmir has the distinction of being the only State in the country where the process of decentralisation was carried out at the district level by way of constitution of the district development boards.

Through this mechanism, it was proposed to secure the participation of the people through their representatives in the developmental process. The twin objectives of the *Single Line Administration* was to secure a mechanism for developing the planning process at the district level to take full account of the resource endowments, the potentialities and need structure and also to initiate a process of equitable development of the various areas within the district. With the formation of district development boards and the delegation of authority for the planning as well as administration of the schemes at the district level, a process of precocious demand was unleashed in all those areas which had hitherto remained cut off from the centre of power and had no say in the decision-making process. Over a period of time it had been very difficult to contain the spate of demands due to the constraint of resources, both financial and of personnel. The problems have got further accentuated because of the increased thrust on the rural development programmes with the basic focus on anti-poverty schemes.

It is therefore inevitable both from the political and the administrative angles to support the district development and planning boards with the institutional framework right at the grassroots level to channellise the flow of serried demands and to have better structural coordination to ensure that the benefits reach the people in the requisite measure. The trends are discernible, though these have occurred in an inchoate and segmented manner not susceptible to any rational explanation. But if deeper insight is given to what has been happening in the rural areas because of the major thrust on rural developmental activities, one would be struck by a tremendous strength and force emerging at the grassroots level which needs to be properly channellised and coordinated. For want of better expression or dispersal of area of influence, these forces tend to take digressive and dissipated tendencies, which at times have also assumed law and order overtones. It is, therefore, increasingly felt that the human potential which is available at the grassroots level should be mainstreamed into the movement of development to purvey a sound and strong basis to the democratic structure. It is in this context that the desire to have a sound institutional framework to give a definite and positive role to the community in the matter of self-governance, has provided a sense of urgency for restructuring the institutional framework of panchayati raj. The Panchayati Raj Act which has been passed by the Jammu and Kashmir Legislature, therefore, is the culmination of the need to reflect the demand structure felt on the ground by purveying the right kind of institution for actualising the objective of democratic decentralisation and participatory administration below the district level.

Briefly, the main plank of the structure proposed through the Jammu and Kashmir Panchayati Raj Act proposes a three-tier system at the halqa, block and district levels. The main strength of the said Act lies in providing a very strong structure at the grassroots level where not only the members of the panchayati halqa are elected but even the sarpanch of the halqa is proposed to be directly elected. At the block level, there has been a change in the structure from the one conceived at the time of the introduction of the Bill which provided for the direct election of the chairman of the block development council. The Act provides for indirect election of the chairman by the elected members of all the halqas in a block. There has not been any perceptible change in the tier at the district level which was conceived originally as a part of the *Single Line Administration*. The structural aspect as envisaged in the Act has been a source of critical debate for it does not provide for the accepted concept of democratisation in terms of acquiescence to the predominant role of the people to decide about the organisational structure at every tier of the proposed framework. However, the strength of the system and the structure should be evaluated or judged from the standpoint of the cultural ethos and the specialised requirements of a particular State and not in terms of any uniform pattern or model. So long as the objective is to secure increasingly the participation of the people both in the decision-making process as well as for the purpose of monitoring the various programme of activities which have a bearing on the improvement in community life as well as in the quality of life, the basic and fundamental objective has been achieved.

The legislation to provide for the structure of the institutional framework has achieved the basic component of the process and the movement towards democratic decentralisation. Once the euphoria over better role performance for the community as manifested through a process of legislation settles down, the real test of the efficacy of the system would be tried out. The various problems which are likely to be set the implementation of the process of democratic decentralisation on the ground are being dealt with in this particular article. This is only by way of pointing out the pitfalls from the practical considerations which must be avoided if fair and meaningful operationalisation of the scheme is visualised:

1. Once the instrument is available with the government for realisation of the theme of democratic decentralisation, it would be essential to see that these institutions actually achieve the objectives. The speed with which the whole process is translated into the action frame would stabilise and strengthen the hope of the community. It is only through the process of bringing these institutions into existence that the process of resurrection of faith of the society in self-governance would be ushered.
2. Another vital dimension is the attitudinal factor governing the institutionalisation of the framework. Unless the structure is viewed as an important tool for sharing of power at different levels, the scheme would never really take off. Given the base for experimentation as well as the historical perspective governing the conceptual aspect of erstwhile panchayati institutions, it is important that right attitudes are developed and evolved to firm up the basis for the new structure. In contradistinction to the accepted philosophy of treating the local

bodies as a mere instrument for effecting administrative delegation of authority and for devolution of the planning process, the whole scheme has to be conceived as a device for sharing of political power. This implies recognition of the capacity and capabilities of the people to influence effectively the decision-making process and to cede to them the sense of participation in the developmental process. How best these institutions would be pulled out of the realm of rhetoric and brought on the plane of reality, would require a drastic transformation in the orientation and attitude towards the institutional framework. Democratic decentralisation is to be construed as a political instrument rather than a mere administrative play.

This is the area where the view is completely smogged at present. If these institutions become cosmetic bodies to carry out the developmental programmes on the same lines with the predominance of the official representatives, then the underlying fundamental objective of conceiving such institutions would be nullified.

The acceptance of the system as an instrument of devolution of political power alone can ensure the successful implementation of the scheme for which this revolutionary and innovative legislation has been enacted. The political orientation to make the panchayati institutions as important bodies both for exercise of administrative as well as political powers would determine the efficacy and the usefulness of these institutions as an effective system for bringing about socio-politico-economic change. It is through the realisation of making these institutions as the basis for political transformation that the future course of development of the process would be determined. This would require proper orientation and attitudinal changes at the political level to give a fair trial to the operation of the system.

3. Another critical area would be the relationship which is likely to emerge between the administrative authorities and the people's representatives at the three tiers of the institutional framework. Apart from that, the relationship of the MLA with the chairman of the block development council as well as the blending of the various institutions to provide an integrated approach are the other crucial areas. The very fact

that the original proposition for having the chairman of the block development council directly elected was substituted by an indirectly elected chairman, reflects some sort of inhibition, a sense of caution or circumspection which has been exercised by the legislators in finalising the shape of the institutional framework for the purpose of achievement of the goal of democratic decentralisation. With the implementation of this scheme and the institutionalisation of the framework, the role of the MLA *vis-a-vis* the chairman of the BDC shall have to be redefined. There is a tremendous possibility of conflict and tension emerging because of the divergence of interests at these two levels. More so as the existence of the chairman of BDC at the block level would be perceived by the MLA as leading to diminution of the role or all pervasive area of influence hitherto-fore exercise by him. This would call for a proper delineation and understanding to develop and evolve between the MLA and the chairman of the block development council to avoid any friction or divergence which would be counter-productive. There would be a tendency on the part of the chairman of the BDC to zealously safeguard the new vistas of power or the area of influence thereby reducing the importance of MLA in that role which had been donned by him for want of any other institution below the district level. Without a positive stance from the MLA, there would be tremendous difficulty in smooth operation of the scheme. However, commitment on the part of the MLA and his active support would create a better understanding all through the line. The MLA should have the opportunity to get involved in major decision-making processes rather than getting bogged down to the detailed aspects of implementation. This is the most difficult part to achieve because the MLA shall have to reflect deeply on his new and entirely different role than the one so far carried out by him. MLAs had perceived their role more in the context of local problems, day to day matters which brought them in direct contact with the electorate. Now their intervention in local matters would be much less and in this process MLAs are likely to get a feeling of being distanced from the community. Initially, therefore, there would be resistance, tension and friction which had to be evened out with better perceptual clarity of the rules of the game.

Anyway this is a critical area which would determine the efficacy of the institutions at the block and the district levels.

4. Allied to this is the redefinition of the role of the administrative authorities who had dominated developmental scenario for all these years. Though the newly-evolved system would still provide a predominant role for the administrative authorities in terms of development of projects, conceptualisation of schemes, working out modalities for the implementation of the programmes and also the execution of the scheme — they shall have to concede their basic accountability to the representatives of the people with regard to decision-making. Officials, because of their access to the data base and information system, shall continue to exercise a much more vital role in this process. It is here that a proper orientation has to be induced to see that the administrative machinery is able to inform the decision-makers about all the ingredients and the data involved. In the initial years, the role to be performed by the administrators would be very vital and critical but once the people's representatives are grounded in the mechanics of decision-making, a new role proposition shall have to emerge between the administrators and the politicians. There is a possibility of friction between the administrators and the politicians. But once the roles crystallise and the people's representatives are better experienced in the dynamics of the process, a definite change would emerge.
5. The success of the system would depend upon the financial resources available at different levels to instil the feeling of self-dependence in these institutions. It is expected that as a part of evolutionary process there would be a demand for discretion and authority to plan the schemes and programmes to decide intersectoral priorities rather than being constricted within the confines of the sectoral planning framework. These institutions if given full support would emerge as the bedrock of democratic principles. It would then be difficult to circumscribe their involvement to the extent of deciding the locational aspects of the schemes, of having the programmes fixed and having the amounts tied down to the earmarked sectors. These would not be able to contain and sustain the unleashed requirements and the demand structure from the grassroots level. This would induce the changes in the plan-

ning structure where the decision-making would have to be real and effective.

6. The institution proposed at the district level leaves a lot of scope for manipulative tendencies from the centre of power. Depending upon the political structure at the grassroots level, the State government would have tremendous authority to direct and guide the movement of development rather than leaving greater autonomy in terms of functioning. This is going to be a basic problem since the resource endowment at the panchayat halqa level is not adequate to provide for their independent functioning. The dependence of these institutions on the State government for finances would be a determinant in defining the role to be performed by the State government and the level of autonomy available to these local bodies.
7. Above all, the survival of these institutions and their future evolution hinges on the commitment to and the faith in the system, the level of political maturity, the orientation of the bureaucracy to the new power matrix and a positive effort to make the institutions work as vibrant, dynamic bodies. Mere piece of legislation will not do. It is only a sound approach for making changes in the restructuring of the power base which can establish the credibility of the system. Now, it is for the system to respond to this demand structure and to use it effectively for furthering the objective of democracy.

The expectations roused in the common man have to fructify on the ground, for the sluice now opened cannot be stopped without peril to the system itself. It is now time to take note of the pressure which is simmering underneath the debate on public participation and to deploy it for strengthening democracy.

EIGHT

Panchayati Adalats in the Jammu and Kashmir Legislation

Alice Jacob and M. C. Mehta

THE Constitution, in its Preamble, seeks to secure to all its citizens: "JUSTICE social, economic and political; LIBERTY of thought, expression, belief, faith and worship; EQUALITY of status and opportunity; and to promote among them all FRATERNITY assuring the dignity of the individual and the unity and integrity of the Nation".

To achieve this goal of dignity of the individual with justice, it is imperative that the judicial system be capable of delivering quick justice to the people. Unfortunately our present judicial system has failed to keep pace with the aspirations of the people. Due to inadequate strength of the judiciary, backlog of cases and complicated procedures, the courts in India have become helpless in delivering quick justice and are thus becoming ineffective.

In ancient times a court house was considered the temple of justice but today it is called a court of law. If we have to transform courts to temples of justice inspiring faith amongst the people, it is essential that panchayat adalats/nyaya panchayats start functioning at the grass roots level to deliver efficacious, cheap and prompt justice.

In some parts of China judges reportedly move their desks from court rooms to residential neighbourhoods where they strive to settle their cases on the spot.[1]

Judges of a district court in Shanghai have started making house calls to help settle disputes. This experiment has been a considerable success. The new practice not only saves people from the trouble of going to court but also simplifies the legal procedure.

In 1942 Mahatma Gandhi elaborated the concept of village *swaraj* in the following terms:

> My idea of village Swaraj is that it is a complete republic, independent of its neighbours for its vital wants and yet interdependent for many others in which dependence is a necessity. Thus every village's first concern will be to grow its own food-crops and cotton for its cloth. It should have a reserve for its cattle, recreation and playgrounds for its adults and children. Then if there is more land available, it will grow useful money crops. The village will maintain a village theatre, school and public hall. It will have its own water works ensuring clean supply. Education will be compulsory up to the final basic course. As far as possible every activity will be conducted on cooperative basis. There will be a compulsory service of village guards, who will be selected by rotation from the register maintained by the village. The government of the village will be conducted by the panchayat of 5 persons elected annually by the adult villagers, male and female both possessing minimum prescribed qualifications. These will have all the authority and jurisdiction required. This panchayat will be legislature, judiciary and executive combined, to operate for its year of office. Any village can become such a republic today without much interference.[2]

In 1946, he again reiterated that panchayats, the rural self-governing units, be entrusted with the task of dispensing justice and subordinate judges asked to go to the villages and assist panchayats in deciding cases.

In India a forum for resolution of disputes with people's participation in the administration of justice is the constitutional goal mandated by Article 39A of the Constitution. Article 39A directs the State to secure that the operation of the legal system promotes justice, on the basis of equal opportunity and shall in particular provide free legal aid, by suitable legislation or schemes or in any other way, to ensure that opportunities for securing justice are not denied to any citizen on the ground of economic or other disabilities. The Constitution now mandates us to remove impediments to access to justice in a systematic manner. Article 40 which directs the State to take steps to organise village panchayats and endow them with such powers and authorities as to enable them to function as units of self-government, has to be interpreted afresh in the light of the new mandate in Article 39A.

In the past, in the organisation of nyaya panchayats, the predominant consideration had been to reduce the burden on the State court system and not so much as to prevent denial of justice because of economic and other disabilities. The "other disabilities" referred to in Article 39A as distinct from the economic disabilities are those which arise from the profiles of the Indian legal system because of absence of suitable local, grass roots organs for handling disputes and emphasising on professionalised justice. Professionalised justice, with the lawyers dominating the process of the justice-delivery system cannot be extended to the bulk of Indian masses in the rural areas because most of the 2,50,000 lawyers are concentrated in urban areas. Moreover, given the voluntary nature of the profession, they cannot be dispersed to adequately and equitably serve the needs of the Indian masses.[3]

New people's courts or tribunals — not merely procedural alterations are envisaged in Article 39A to ensure a new legal system and procedure which is operationally geared to social justice and elimination of all disabilities of the masses in getting real, remedial justice. The ends are social and economic justice, the means are legal remedies; the parameters are equal opportunity for the masses to reach remedies. Panchayati raj with full powers of functional self-government, is mandated by Article 40. Self-government must include judicial powers too and that is the rationale for panchayati adalats or nyaya panchayats which implies judicial decentralism at the people's level.[4] Effective access to justice may be seen as the most basic requirement, the most basic 'human right' of a system which purports to guarantee legal rights.[5]

These grass roots level judicial institutions represent the secular, equalitarian, modernistic legal ideology thus assisting the desired social transformation. The Law Commission in its Fourteenth Report stresses the "educative value of nyaya panchayats"; just as the village panchayats would educate the villager in the art of self-government "so would nyaya panchayats" train him in the art of doing justice between fellow citizens and instil in him a growing sense of fairness and responsibility. In this respect, nyaya panchayats constitute an aspect of overall development.

These panchayati adalats/nyaya panchayats constitute a sub-system of the State administration of justice as well as a sub-system of panchayats. For example, in relation to constitution, finances and secretariat, they constitute a sub-system of panchayats; in their actual operation they are a sub-system of the State apparatus of justice.

The institutions represent the extension of the State's legal system in the rural areas. The extension of State law means extension of the political system as well. This is attempted to be done through structuring nyaya panchayats in such a manner as would combine some features, for example, formal principles of organisation and operation, hierarchy, oversight and control of the State legal system with some other prominent features of community dispute-handling processes (e.g., informality, flexibility), etc. This makes these institutions half-way institutions between full-fledged judicial institutions of the State on the one hand and those "judicial" institutions which flourish under the auspices of the communities themselves without the aid of law or State, on the other.

II

The Jammu and Kashmir legislation aims at revitalising panchayati raj institutions including the panchayati adalats. It provides the evolution of a system which promises quick relief without cumbersome formalities and heavy expenditure.

Composition

The Jammu and Kashmir Panchayati Raj Bill, 1988, envisages a panchayati adalat for every halqa which consists of a contiguous number of villages as determined by the government [S. 42(1)]. The adalat is to consist of three members nominated by the prescribed authority out of the panel prepared and recommended by the halqa panchayat from its electorate [S. 42(2)]. The term of members of the adalat is five years [S. 42(3)]. Two members will form the quorum [S. 42(4)].

The chairman of the adalat is to be elected by the members of the adalat from amongst themselves. If they fail to elect within 15 days, the prescribed authority will nominate the chairman (S. 44).

The secretary of the halqa panchayat, namely, the village level worker will act as the judicial clerk to the adalat (S. 45).

Jurisdiction

Panchayati adalats enjoy both criminal and civil jurisdictions.

The criminal jurisdiction is extensive and covers a substantial range of offences under the Ranbir Panel Code, 1989, as well as the special statutes such as the Cattle Trespass Act, 1977; the Jammu and Kashmir Vaccination Act, 1990; the Gambling Act, 1977 and the Prevention of Juvenile Smoking Act, 1986. The Panchayati adalats have jurisdiction to try offences such as affray, impersonation of public servant, criminal trespass, house trespass, public nuisance including pollution of water, mischief, theft, misappropriation (subject to a pecuniary limit of Rs. 100), criminal intimidation, absconding to evade service of summons, rash and negligent driving on a highway, outrage etc. (S. 50 and First Schedule). The adalat is authorised to levy a fine up to a maximum of Rs. 1,000 but it has no power to sentence offenders to imprisonment (S. 52). The adalat is empowered to pay compensation to the victims of offences out of the fine imposed on the offenders (S. 53). It is also empowered to order the complainant to compensate the accused up to Rs. 200 in case of false, frivolous or vexatious complaints (S. 54). It has the power to discharge a youthful offender (not over 15 years of age) after admonition.

Civil jurisdiction is confined to claims of the value of Rs. 1,000 involving suits for ascertained sums, for damages for breach of contract not involving immovable property, compensation for wrongful taking or damaging property [S. 61(1)]. The Government is empowered to enhance the jurisdiction in civil cases up to Rs. 2,000 [S. 62(2)].

The adalat is empowered to arbitrate between parties where the value of the suit does not exceed Rs. 2,000 (S. 71).

Simplicity of procedures and flexibility of functioning are two essential features of lay adjudication. The provisions of the Code of Civil Procedure, 1977, the Code of Criminal Procedure, 1989, Court Fees Act, 1977, the Evidence Act, 1977 and Limitation Act, 1895 are not applicable to proceedings before the adalat (S. 76). Lawyers are barred from appearing on behalf of parties before the adalat (S. 102). It has the power to compound an offence under the Act

(S. 100). Further, it may permit any case to be compounded if it is according to the provisions of the Cr. P.C., 1989. Similarly, the adalat is empowered to take steps to reach an amicable settlement of suits which is in consonance with nyaya panchayat ideology (S. 80).

The chairman and the members of the adalat are entitled to a sitting fee (S. 102). They cannot hold any formal position within the village panchayats [S. 42(2)]. Consequently, they are isolated from the power hierarchy of village societies; also they are not tenured members of the judicial service.

Salutary Features of the Bill

(i) The jurisdiction conferred on the adalat is exclusive to the extent that in respect of matters covered by the jurisdiction conferred on the adalat, the jurisdiction of any other court is ousted, unless a reference to a regular competent court is made by the adalat itself (Ss. 70 and 81). In other words, the jurisdiction conferred is not optional. This is as it should be if the adalats are to be strengthened as lay adjudicators.

(ii) Appeals are barred both in civil and criminal cases against the decisions or sentences of the adalat. Instead, revision to a district court or sessions court on questions of legality or propriety of the decree or sentence passed by the adalat is provided for (S. 84). As the ideology of the adalat is adjudication by one's own peers, the ban of appeal ensures generation of faith and confidence in their decision-making process. Moreover, provisions for appeal cannot necessarily cure all errors. But revision on questions of law may ensure prevention of miscarriage of justice. However, this power of revision has also to be used sparingly and not on grounds that if the revisional authority would have appreciated questions of fact, it would have decided otherwise. Only errors of law should come within the revisional jurisdiction.

(iii) The criminal jurisdiction is quite extensive.

Suggestions

The civil jurisdiction may be enlarged to cover specifically non-payment of wages and violation of Minimum Wages Act; disputes arising out of the partnership in cultivation of land; disputes on the usc of forcst producc by local inhabitants; disputes regarding use of common pasture, and disputes concerning regulation and timing of taking water from irrigation channels.

The revitalisation of the panchayat adalat should also involve measures for improving the quality of justice administered by the adalats—qualities of impartiality, fairness in decision-making processes and equality in enforcement of decrees and sentences regardless of the socio-economic status of the parties.[6] Further, the members of the adalats must be trained to administer justice according to the law.[7] Legal literacy programmes should be arranged for them. The law faculties of Jammu and Kashmir universities may be mobilised to conduct para-legal programmes for the members of the adalats.

NOTES

1. "China takes courts to people", *IIPA Newsletter*, June, 1983, Vol. XXVII, No. 6, p. 8.
2. *Harijan*, 26th July, 1942.
3. See Law Commission of India, One Hundred and Fourteenth Report on *Gram Nyayalaya*, 15-16 (1986).
4. See generally Justice V. R. Krishna Iyer, *Our Courts on Trial* (BRPC, Delhi, 1987).
5. See Cappelletti, Mauro and Garth, Bryant, (ed.), *Access to Justice* (4 volumes), 1978-79.
6. See for an exhaustive and incisive analysis of nyaya panchayats, Upendra Baxi, "Access, Development and Distributive Justice", Vol. 18, *Journal of the Indian Law Institute* 375 at 411-430 (1976).
7. The Law Commission of India (Fourteenth Report on *Reform of Judicial Administration* (1958); Government of India, Report of the Study Team on Nyaya Panchayats (1962).

NINE

Financial Problems of Panchayati Raj Institutions: The J & K Case

Abhijit Datta

Introduction

THE present state of panchayati raj in Jammu and Kashmir is somewhat uncertain due to paucity of detailed, reliable, and up to date information. After Independence, there have been two panchayati raj legislations in the State in 1951 and 1958 and now the State Assembly is considering passage of another Bill to remodel the panchayats. Jammu and Kashmir has a single-tier system at the halqa level covering 4.7 villages having an average population of 3,218 with a total number of halqa panchayats being 1,469. It is claimed that the State has covered its entire rural population through the halqa panchayats, though all these have been superseded for a long time without any State assistancee in support of their revenues.

The sources of revenue for the halqa panchayats as provided in the Jammu and Kashmir Village Panchayat Act, 1958 include the following:

i. Taxes: on professions, animals and vehicles, hired boats, pilgrims, etc.;
ii. Non-tax revenue: rates on water and lighting; fees on graz-

ing cattle etc., and realisations from community assets and
iii. State assistance: assignment of sanitation cess (at the rate of 3 per cent on land revenue), grants and advances.

The actual income position of the halqa panchayats are as shown in Table 1.

Table 1

Revenue Income of Panchayats in Jammu and Kashmir

	(Rs lakh) 1978-79	1979-80
(i) Taxes	36.71	36.71
(ii) Non-tax revenue	17.94	73.26
(iii) State assistance	--	--
TOTAL	54.65	109.97
	Rs	Rs
Average per halqa panchayat	37.20	74.86
Per capita halqa panchayat	1.16	2.32

Source: *Panchayati Raj at a Glance: 1981-82* (Government of India, Ministry of Rural Development), New Delhi, 1983.

From Table 1 it appears that the tax income has remained constant, while the non-tax revenue has increased substantially, and that the State government has not been providing any revenue assistance to the panchayats. Assuming that the increase in non-tax revenue in 1979-80 was unusual, we may take 1978-79 pattern as normal.

The new Jammu and Kashmir Panchayati Raj Bill, 1988 may substantially alter the situation through: (a) the introduction of two additional tiers of panchayati raj institutions (PRIs) at the block and district levels, and (b) introduction of a well-conceived system of fiscal transfers to the PRI. Therefore, it is important to examine the provisions of the Bill, especially the fiscal arrangements of the three-tier panchayats and the policy on fiscal transfers to the PRIs. Afterwards, it would be appropriate to make some suggestions on the financial management of the PRIs. Finally, we would attempt to highlight the main thrusts of the paper in a concluding section.

Fiscal Arrangements for the PRIs

a. *Tax Powers*

In order to discharge their functions adequately and to inculcate a sense of fiscal responsibility in the new PRIs, it is desirable that at least the block development councils (BDCs) are accorded taxation powers so that a substantial part of their recurring expenditure could be financed through their own revenues. Such taxes could be property tax, trade and professions tax, and a cess on land revenues.

b. *Assigned and Shared Taxes*

The Bill provides for the continuance of the existing provision of assignment of the sanitation cess to the halqa panchayats. However, it would also be necessary to consider the possibility of a few State taxes to be either assigned or shared with the district planning and development boards (DPDBs).

c. *Grants*

The Bill provides for a per capita revenue grant to the halqa panchayats and it would be proper to hand over the total allocation for this purpose to the DPDBs only with a provision to redistribute this grant to the BDCs which, in turn, should reallocate this grant to the halqa panchayats, as per norms prescribed for each level of PRIs. A matching condition of internal tax revenues could be introduced to encourage local revenue mobilisation. It would also be necessary to provide for a statutory Panchayati Raj Finance Commission, once in five years, to recommend an appropriate volume of fiscal transfers to the PRIs at various levels and finally to the individual bodies. It would be appropriate to channel all State fiscal assistance to the PRIs through DPDBs.

d. *Loans*

The Bill is silent about the allocation of loans from government and other financial institutions for development purposes. This needs to be linked with proper preparation of development plans by all the three tiers of the PRIs and arrangements of their financing. Without this, the present uncertainty of external fiscal support and lack of fiscal commitment on the part of the PRIs to finance local development schemes and projects would continue.

e. *Fiscal Tiering*

Keeping these above-mentioned objectives in mind, it is suggested that the fiscal profile of the three tiers of the PRIs in the State may be made as under:

1. *Halqa Panchayats*

— a capitation (or poll) tax may replace the professional tax to finance village-level development projects.
— net collection of the sanitation cess may be made over to the halqa panchayats by the State revenue authorities.
— the percapita grant allocations to the halqa panchayats may be made by the BDCs on a matching formula based on their tax collection performance.
— development assistance to the halqa panchayats is to be made to them by the BDCs on a matching formula depending upon their contribution to finance the approved halqa development plans.

2. *Block Development Councils*

— BDCs should be empowered to impose house tax and cesses thereon — the cesses are to finance major public services like, education, roads, public health. Trade and professional taxes should be imposed by the BDCs instead of the halqa panchayats as at present.
— the net collection of a new cess on land revenue should accrue to the BDCs.
— revenue grants to the BDCs are to be allocated by the

DPDBs on a matching basis, as for the halqa panchayats.

— development assistance to the BDCs is to be allocated by the DPDBs on a matching basis, as for the halqa panchayats.

3. *District Planning and Development Boards*

— net collection of a future entry tax for the district is to be assigned to the DPDBs; 50 per cent share of some of the State taxes (net collection in the districts) like, motor vehicles tax, entertainment tax, stamp duty, are to be paid to the DPDBs.

— revenue grants are to be made to the DPDBs on a matching basis, as for the BDCs and halqa panchayats.

— development assistance, covering both Plan transfers and institutional support to the DPDBs, is to be made on a matching basis, as for the BDCs and halqa panchayats.

— all State fiscal transfers, both Plan and non-Plan, to the PRIs are to be routed through the DPDBs.

— a statutory quinquennium Panchayati Raj Finance Commission should be appointed to recommend the volume of fiscal transfers to the PRIs.

Policy on Fiscal Transfers

a. *Current Situation*

At present, the State governments do not have any firm policy of fiscal transfers to the PRIs. Allocations made are also too meagre and somewhat uncertain, in spite of elaborate grants codes governing them in some of the States. *Annexure* shows that in the smaller States, the average level of united fiscal transfers comes to 0.1 per cent of their revenue expenditure, with Jammu and Kashmir having no transfers at all. In the larger States also less than 1 per cent of State's revenue expenditure is distributed to the local bodies by way of united grants. It is therefore necessary to fix a firm target of general-purpose fiscal transfers to the local bodies, including the PRIs. Within the next five years, our suggested target is 1 per cent for the less populated States, and 5 per cent for the more populated States in this regard. The PRI share could be about a third of this target, leaving the rest for the municipal authorities. It is somewhat unrealistic to assume that the States would in the forseeable future transfer 50 per cent of their total revenue expenditure to the PRIs, as earlier envisaged by the Asoka Mehta Committee.[1]

b. *Transfer Machinery*

It is important to view the Plan and non-Plan fiscal transfers to the PRI together on the basis of certain norms and criteria decided at a policy level of the State Government. Creation of PRI finance commissions at periodic intervals, as suggested earlier, would be helpful in this regard. This can be done if the State Planning Board could be involved in the process for finalising the district plans and assessing the fiscal capabilities of the PRI for their financing, in the same manner as the State Plan allocations are finalised by the Planning Commission. The PRI Finance Commission, likewise, could adopt the same methods to estimate the required volume of grant-in-aid of PRI revenue. Shared and assigned State taxes to the PRIs are to be statutorily fixed to remove uncertainties in the release of their net receipts to the PRIs.

c. *Revenue Transfers*

The per capita grant to be distributed to the halqa panchayats will have to be substantial to reach the all-India levels as reported by the Asoka Mehta Committee for 1976-77 and reproduced in Table 2.

It is clear from Table 2 that a simple per capita grant will not be able to meet the committed expenditures of the halqa panchayats so that it has to be supplemented by deficit grants and function-specific grants. Allocations of general grants—both per capita and deficit grants—would have to be related to local tax efforts and the recurring expenditure requirements of the PRIs at all levels.

Apart from grants, the other two elements of States' fiscal transfers relate to tax assignment and tax-sharing. Here also policy decisions are needed about the taxes to be assigned and shared. Broadly speaking, a 50 per cent sharing on various bases may be adopted. The fiscal transfers should not in any way dampen the tax efforts and fiscal responsibility of the PRIs in view of their larger transfer requirements.

Table 2

Revenue Income of Panchayats, 1976-77

Levels	Percentages				Per capita (Rs)
	Tax	Non-tax	Grants	Total	
J & K halqa panchayats	63.3	36.7		100	0.2
All-India					
(18 States) Gram Panchayats	34.8	18.2	47.0	100	10.4
(12 States) Panchayat Samitis	14.2	0.2	85.6	100	1.6
(6 States) Zilla Parishads	6.8	1.2	92.0	100	0.2
					12.2

Source: *Report of the Committee on Panchayati Raj Institutions*, op. cit., pp. 279-92.

Financial Management

a. *PRI Executive*

The Bill is somewhat weak in delineating the executive arrangements in the proposed PRIs in the State. It is necessary to spell out the distribution of executive decision-making process in greater detail. This would also clarify the relationship between the appointed chief executives and the respective chairmen of all the three tiers of the PRI.

b. *Budget and Scrutiny of Expenditure*

A statutory finance committee of the elected members, along with a time-bound programme of budget and audit of the PRIs may have to be incorporated to ensure financial responsibility, propriety and accountability. Proper accounting and budget formats are also to be framed subsequently under the rules. The recommendations of the Santhanam Committee is relevant in this regard, namely:

> The ordinary recurring receipts on the income side and the normal committed expenditure on the disbursement side

should be kept separate from receipts and expenditure of a capital nature so that panchayat may be aware whether it is solvent or not.[2]

It would also be necessary to specify appropriate financial management practices in the PRIs through relevant rules and ensure their compliance through adequate State supervision. It is necessary to specify the distribution of tax powers and provide for assignment and sharing of State taxes to the PRIs so that all the three tiers could be assured of a minimum degree of financial autonomy necessary to maintain local services and undertake local projects. In addition, there is a need to frame proper policies for allocation and dusbursement of State grants and Plan assistance to the PRIs for budgetary support and implementation of their own Plans and projects. The overall thrust would be to ensure financial solvency, along with promotion of fiscal responsibility, of the PRIs in Jammu and Kashmir.

NOTES

1. *Report of the Committee on Panchayati Raj Institutions* (India: Ministry of Agriculture and Irrigation), New Delhi, 1978.

2. *Report of the Study Team on Panchayati Raj Finances* (India: Ministry of Community Development and Cooperation), New Delhi, 1983, p. 41.

Annexure

States' United Fiscal Transfers to Local Bodies: 1987-88 (BE)

	States Group A (Population of less than 1 crore)	Total Revenue Expenditure (TRE) (Rs. Crore)	Transfers to Local Bodies (TLB) (Rs. Crore)	Percentage of TLB to TRE	TLB at 1 per cent of TRE (Rs. Crore)
1.	Himachal Pradesh	494.74	2.25	0.5	4.95
2.	**Jammu & Kashmir**	**743.47**	**0.00**	**0.0**	**7.43**
3.	Manipur	197.28	0.00	0.0	1.97
4.	Meghalaya	185.17	0.00	0.0	1.85
5.	Mizoram	148.91	0.00	0.0	1.49
6.	Nagaland	267.31	0.00	0.0	2.67
7.	Sikkim	85.90	0.00	0.0	0.86
8.	Tripura	275.99	1.48	0.5	2.76
	Average	299.85	0.47	0.1	3.00
	Group B (Population of 1 crore and above)				**TLB at 5 per cent of TRE (Rs. Crore)**
1.	Andhra Pradesh	3728.57	43.35	1.2	186.43
2.	Assam	1259.59	6.80	0.5	62.98
3.	Bihar	2537.84	10.64	0.4	126.89
4.	Gujarat	2677.73	14.98	0.6	133.89
5.	Haryana	1084.34	0.42	...	54.22
6.	Karnataka	2706.56	62.36	2.3	135.33
7.	Kerala	1733.37	0.98	0.1	86.67
8.	Madhya Pradesh	2968.22	57.28	1.9	148.41
9.	Maharashtra	5351.88	22.97	0.4	267.59
10.	Orissa	1410.00	7.10*	0.5	70.50
11.	Punjab	1351.00	11.86	0.9	67.55
12.	Rajasthan	1934.88	7.19	0.4	96.74
13.	Tamil Nadu	2874.00	30.85	...	143.70
14.	Uttar Pradesh	4924.51	34.70	0.7	246.23
15.	West Bengal	2942.24	97.38	3.3	147.11
	Average	2632.32	27.26	0.9	131.62

Note: . . . = negligible; 0 = nil, * = includes Plan expenditure (Rs. 1.82 crores)
Source: *Reserve Bank of India Bulletin*, October 1987.

TEN

Poverty Alleviation requires More Attention

Mohammad Sultan

POVERTY alleviation has, of late, come to be regarded as a strategic factor in the development process in India. During the Fifties and early Sixties it was conceived to be almost synonymous with agricultural growth. The hypothesis was based on the premise that sustained agricultural growth would automatically make a dent on rural poverty through the "trickle-down" mechanism. However, the failure of higher agricultural rates of growth to reduce, even marginally, the magnitude of rural poverty, persuaded the decision-makers to recast their perceptions. Disenchantment with earlier optimism in fact started in the mid-Sixties itself. It was felt that the tolerance of rural poverty had the potential of undermining the very process of development in the country and that a proportionate and balanced growth of urban and rural sectors was a necessary condition for a sustained and satisfactory growth of the national economy.

There are differences of opinion among planners, policy-makers and experts about the operational meaning and definition of the poverty line. But by and large a broad consensus has emerged that a man and his family of four to five members must have an income of Rs 6,400 a year (at current prices) to be able to meet the minimum consumption requirements. All those below this norm are defined as poor. Those with annual income of less than Rs 4,800 are defined as very poor and those with only up to Rs 3,500 are the poorest of the poor.

The Government of India holds that the number of the poor is below 300 million (60-65 million families). But many scholars argue that the number is nearly 400 million (80-85 million families).

The Government of India launched numerous programmes from time to time to uplift the rural poor so that the syndrome that entangles them could be broken and the decks cleared for raising their incomes and levels of living. All these programmes were launched with the twin objectives of giving a boost to the national economy and reducing poverty. Some of the most important programmes chalked out in this context were: (i) Small Farmers Development Agency (SFDA); (ii) Marginal Farmers and Agricultural Labourers Programme (MFAL); (iii) Drought-Prone Area Programme (DPAP); (iv) Integrated Rural Development Programme (IRDP); (v) National Rural Employment Programme (NREP); and (vi) TRYSEM. All these programmes were conceptualised and formulated on the explicit assumption of decentralised planning.

Considerable efforts have been made by the Central and State governments to reduce the incidence of rural poverty through these schemes. However, the results have not been commensurate with the efforts that have been made. Even the decentralised and multi-level planning process has yet to emerge as a viable mechanism in the country. There is enough evidence to suggest that the lack of effective decentralisation has hampered the implementation of anti-poverty programmes. However, at the conceptual level, the villain of the piece is the very conception of poverty which smacks of a "gross category approach". This approach does not take into consideration the deprivation suffered by the absolutely poor within the poverty segment. Generally the Rowntree-Bewridge concept of poverty has found favour with the decision-makers. Accordingly, the strategies formulated violate the basics of both poverty alleviation programmes and decentralised planning.

Studies on poverty and poverty alleviation strategies[1] across the country/regions/districts/blocks reveal that poverty continues to be a function of:

1. Concentration of power—economic, political, social and bureaucratic.
2. Monopolisation of resources and markets by a ruthless lumpen middle class and rural elite which shares the booty in the name of poverty alleviation.
3. Lop-sided socio-economic research for conceptualising poverty and formulating effective policies for its removal.

4. Gradual decline of rural institutions and lackadaisical efforts to build new institutions which could act as agents of social transformation.
5. Scale-biased and area-biased agricultural transformation coupled with rising cost of agricultural output.
6. Irrational use of resources, particularly land, water, flora, fauna and forests.
7. Introduction and perpetuation of an organisational setup for rural development which is oriented towards a Centrally guided service-delivery approach.
8. Absence of organised labour movements among rural poor and underemployed.
9. Inappropriate bureaucratic orientation in participatory development.
10. Lack of local-specific strategies and appropriate administrative-cum-delivery mechanisms.
11. Identification of poverty alleviation with expenditure resulting into beneficiaries being cashed-in to fulfil targets.
12. Almost non-existent up to date data collection, monitoring, evaluation, concurrent evaluation and auditing systems at the grassroots level.
13. Highly aggregative and stereotyped methods of identification of: the poor, schemes and solutions under poverty alleviation programmes like IRDP.
14. Minimal integration between core and sectoral investments.
15. Lack of adequate resources for poverty alleviation programmes.

Accordingly most of the studies[2] suggest that:

1. Skewed distribution of assets and wealth must be restructured in favour of the *disadvantaged*. Special *patterns* of *State intervention* and *people's participation* will facilitate access of the poor to markets, employment and viable avenues of income.
2. Accelerated agricultural production is central to poverty eradication. This requires intensive agricultural research and its quick extension, enhanced investment in infrastructure and people's institutions to spread the new technology. Radical institutional changes and viable people's institutions are as important as technological changes.

3. Effective population education, to reduce the rates of population growth, and increase in non-agricultural employment avenues to absorb population in rural areas. There is a huge potential for diversification of agriculture to generate new employment avenues.

The equitable distribution of assets and decontrol of resources from the rural elite via people's participation are necessary preconditions for alleviation of poverty. However, in spite of policy prescriptions and constitutional mandates[3] the process of institution-building is at a somewhat nascent stage.[4] Much of the institution-building for rural development continues to be a *trial and error* method. The nagging question is how to create people's institutions which will supplement planning for poverty alleviation?

Two approaches — paternalistic and populistic — have dominated the thinking about rural institutions. "Both are fallacious as these are derived from and based on unreal stereotypes of rural people who are neither as passive and ignorant as assumed in the first approach nor as virtuous and wise as assumed in the second. On the whole, rural people are more capable and responsive than the paternalistic model assumes but less capable to change their lives autonomously than the populistic model assumes.[5]" What is needed is an institution-building mechanism which is neither *top-down* nor *bottom-up* nor exclusively *governmental. Centralised* and *decentralised planning* are not necessarily antagonistic to each other. In fact, these have been conceived as complementary processes in our federal polity. There are of course many areas of economic activity which call for action at the Central level, as, indeed there are areas which call for planning and implementation at the State, district, block and village levels.

The debate on *top-down* or *bottom-up* planning is irrelevant as both are neither inimical to each other nor to rural development. What is needed is the resurgence of each in its proper perspective in a single framework. There is no short-cut to rural development, much less to poverty alleviation. No input to poverty alleviation can be relegated to background.

On this premise, the significance of panchayati raj institutions hardly needs to be restated. Nonetheless, integrating their role in the overall input-matrix of poverty alleviation definitely demands a careful consideration as integration often defies solutions. The problem of integration is to be recast against the backdrop of micro-level planning and federal polity.

Planning for rural transformation means preparing development plans for relatively small and homogeneous areas like blocks, halqas and panchayats. This involves focusing development programmes on the basic needs of village communities and target groups. Given this orientation, the planner has to view the rural area as a social system undergoing diverse processes of change. He has to identify and design the structure and components of micro-level planning. Panchayati raj institutions should automatically become an essential component of this exercise.

II

In consonance with the key role of panchayati raj institutions in poverty alleviation, let us now address ourselves to the Jammu and Kashmir Panchayati Raj Bill, 1988. Political commitment to democratic decentralisation and social justice is not an innovation as far as this State is concerned. Both had been incorporated in the policy outline of *Naya Kashmir*[6] as long ago as 1944 — much before panchayati raj was activised in the States of Rajasthan, Gujarat and Maharashtra in the light of the mandate of Article 40 of the Constitution. Anti-poverty programmes in the State were also articulated by the decision-makers since 1947. A number of agrarian reform measures were introduced to uplift the rural poor from the degradation of poverty, hunger and disease.

In spite of a strong political commitment to democratic decentralisation and social justice, panchayati raj institutions have failed to cross even the embryonic stage. After a long period of suspended animation, these are being reincarnated by the 1988 Panchayati Raj Bill. The Bill is definitely a historic piece of legislation.

The fundamental question underlying all this is whether the Bill has the potential (given the political commitment) to revitalise panchayati raj institutions so that these become viable inputs in the strategies for poverty alleviation in the State. To answer this question it is necessary to refer to the rationale of the Bill as provided in the statement of the objectives. The Bill has been described as a radical step as it aims to, "promote and develop panchayati raj in the State as an instrument of vigorous local self-government to secure the effective participation of the people in the implementation of the development planning". For the effective participation of the rural population in developmental programmes at the grassroots level, the Bill proposes to introduce a three-tier panchayati raj system in the State. These tiers are:

a. Halqa Panchayat;
b. Block Development Council and
c. District Planning and Development Boards.

In its present form, the halqa panchayat is the most crucial tier in the Bill as it provides that the halqa panchayat shall be under *legal duty* to prepare the plans for development of the area and undertake measures for implementation of the development plans. Soil conservation, water management, social forestry, rural industrialisation, various aspects of agriculture and animal husbandry, sanitation and health of the people come under the purview of halqa panchayat. The halqa panchayats are also required to make regulations for the consumer protection and *evolving the programmes for poverty and harnessing the avenues of employment generation through new programmes.*

It is obvious that planning for poverty alleviation and employment generation is one of the major functions of halqa panchayats. It is definitely an innovation and marked improvement over the West Bengal and Karnataka models of panchayati raj. However, the Bill does not provide any formal framework for planning for poverty alleviation at the grassroots level. The real problems always crop up at the implementation stage. To visualise these problems it is essential to elaborate the poverty alleviation function of the halqa panchayats against the backdrop of the present agrarian scene of the State. Institutions cannot be built in vacuum. These invariably reflect the mores of a society. One cannot doubt the intentions of the framers of the present Bill and its historical significance. But it is naive to pass the Bill without appreciating the special challenges which the present agrarian scene of the State is posing. Moreover, taking the Bill beyond the conceptual limitations of panchayati raj institutions is always an over-ambitious legal exercise.

The agrarian structure of the State has undergone significant changes during the past four decades. Besides successful record of land reform measures, Jammu and Kashmir has also attempted to restructure the credit and commodity markets. The restructuring of these markets has had a considerable impact on the organisation and functioning of the commission agents. Consequent upon a set of policy-induced Government interventions in the land market, two distinct and structurally diverse sectors were created: the reform sector — broadly the non-commercial subsistence type agriculture — and the non-reform sector, identifiable with the capitalistically organised commercial sector. The latter is understandably more dynamic and has led to increased investments, facilitated by subsidised credits within the non-reform sector. With the size of land-holding in the reform sector declining due to demographic pressures and urban industrial employment generation being minimal, the non-reform sector has assumed the role of the leading sector in the economy. Consequently, significant changes (which have a bearing on poverty alleviation, labour absorption and pattern of employment) have taken place:

i. The land market is getting distorted with the effective concentration of land having increased over the years.
ii. The agriculture-industry linkages have not been strengthened. On the other hand, agricultural-services linkages (trading linkages) have received a fillip after 1947.
iii. Conventional type of rural-urban migration has gained further momentum along with the emergence of a new type of rural-rural migration, with the migrants effectively alienated from their sustained income-generating assets, particularly land.
iv. The State economy is entirely external market-oriented with no self-sustaining growth impulse generated with the economy.
v. The price structure in the Valley is distorted by the remoteness of the State and partly by the consumers' ignorance. It is quite possible that the regional terms of trade may be against the State economy, particularly in the Valley. Higher prices mean that the purchasing power of the rural population is drained out. This may be a factor in the persistence of poverty.

In this macro-framework, profiling poverty and building institutions assume added complexity. Obviously, this would require an in-depth study of the pattern of economic development in the State in a historical backdrop. This warrants among other things an evaluation of thc observed agricultural growth with particular reference to:

a. Demographic pressures;
b. Non-demographic pressures and
c. State interventions.

Having brought into focus the changes in the agricultural economy an attempt should be made to study the rationale of the nature of interventions to understand the uniqueness of these changes. Despite an increasing demographic pressure, a substantial proportion of land in Kashmir, which increased over time, has been put to the cultivation of non-food crops while foodgrains import intensity for the economy as a whole has increased. The changing trends in: (a) Land-use pattern; (b) Cropping intensity; (c) Cropping pattern; and (d) Consumption levels over time would throw into relief the causes of the higher foodgrains import intensity of the State economy.

It has been observed that there is an effective concentration of land even though absolute concentration of land in big land holdings has declined. The changes in the distribution of land (statistically reflected in either peasants cultivating uneconomic size of holdings and relying on wages as supplementary sources of income or selling land, leading to more concentration of land is a phenomenon that calls for analysis. However, this trend may not be accompanied by the emergence of a high degree of absolute concentration of land in large holdings. It appears that medium-sized orchard holdings play an important role in the agrarian changes in Kashmir. An uneven distribution of holdings in different size category of holdings and a high magnitude of proletarianisation is a disturbing phenomenon of diverse ramifications. What is more disturbing is that these holdings are not found in one compact block. Disparities between rural and urban incomes, between large and small farmers and between wet and dry land cultivators have increased over the years. Programmes of rural prosperity have not been based on intensification and diversification. Almost all the Ph.D. theses conducted on agriculture in Jammu and Kashmir have revealed low income per hectare and low agricultural income per worker and a mismatch between the size and structure of holdings. Consequently, the majority of agricultural holdings in the State have become economically non-viable. Another important reason for small-sized non-economic holdings is perpetual fragmentation and sub-division of holdings. Thus, the present agrarian setup in the State is one of the important causes of rural poverty in Kashmir. The IRDP envisaged covering 66 per cent of schemes in agricultural and related sectors thereby assigning a key role to agricultural transformation in poverty alleviation programmes.

Obviously, the poverty alleviation programmes have to be conceived in a different framework as compared to the all-India pattern. One of the requirements of this framework would call for a disaggregated evaluation of anti-poverty programmes and introduction of a panchayati raj system which will be in harmony with the unique features of rural poverty in Jammu and Kashmir.

Even if we sidetrack these fundamental questions, the following aspects merit special attention:

1. While diverse sectoral plans are being implemented in the specific area, there are at the same time many core programmes being implemented by local authorities under the umbrella of IRDP, NREP, RLEGP, DPAP, etc. Quite frequently one can discern the absence of coordination among different departments operating in the same area and lack of harmony between sectoral and core agencies. The need for decentralised planning and coordination arises specially to correct these drawbacks.

   The halqa panchayat has been visualised as a key instrument of rural planning and poverty alleviation. In addition to its regulatory functions, it has important developmental functions. The formulation and execution of the plans for development of the area within the halqa panchayat is an obligatory function of the local body. Interestingly the primary responsibility of poverty alleviation has been placed on the halqa panchayats. However, a supportive role has been assigned to other tiers also. The halqa panchayat, with its small area and resources would hardly be able to support the manpower needed for planning and execution of its development schemes. The question naturally arises as to how the halqa panchayats will successfully implement plans without any implementing machinery of their own. They cannot support

Hegde, R, "A Basic Standpoint on Centre-State Relations", Institute of Social and Economic Change, Bangalore (mimeographed), 1983.

Hosanain, F M, "British Policy Towards Kashmir", Sterling Publishers, 1947.

Hussain, S I, "The Jammu and Kashmir Agrarian Reforms Act, 1976.

Jha, S P, "Centre-State Finance – Squabbling over Loans and Fishes", *The Times of India*, 1982.

Jose, A M, "Decentralised Planning in India: A Review in the Background of Seventh Five-Year Plan", Institute for Social and Economic Change (ISEC), Bangalore, 1986.

Khan, A M, "People's Participation in Panchayati Raj Institutions", ISEC, Bangalore, 1986.

Kurian, M K, "For Unity in Diversity", ISEC, Bangalore (mimeographed), 1983.

Lawrence Walter, *Valley of Kashmir*, Kesar Publishers, Residency Road, Srinagar.

Mitra, Ashok, "Overdrafts by States, Other Sides of the River", *The Times of India*, 1982.

Mitra, Ashok, "A Symptom of a Deeper Malaria", *The Times of India*, 1982.

Nadkarni, M V, "Underutilisation of productive resources, constraints in their optimum utilisation and possible ways of overcoming them", ISEC, Bangalore (mimeographed), 1986.

Narain, Iqbal, "Panchayati Raj, Democracy and Development in Rural India", in *Peoples Participation in Development Process,* (edited by) Rames K Arora, HCM State Institute of Public Administration, Jaipur, p. 11, 1979.

Nanjundappa, D M, "Decentralised Planning, Problems of Administration and Coordination", ISEC, Bangalore (mimeographed), 1986.

Nirmal, M, "The Alternative District Government", Courtesy: M A Monograph, I L O, Oxford Pub. Co., New Delhi.

Rajindra Arora, "Demographic Trends in Economic Development of Jammu and Kashmir since 1951" (Unpublished).

Ray, A, "Bureaucratic Orientation", ISEC, Bangalore (mimeographed), 1986.

Rao, Hemlata, "Sarkaria Commission and Federal Fiscal Relations", ISEC, Bangalore (mimeographed), 1986.

Rao, K R, "The Federal Process as a Political Process in India", ISEC, Bangalore (mimeographed), 1986.

Rao, V M, "Nature of Rural Development", *EPW,* Vol. XVI, No. 41, October 1981.

Rao, V M, "Data and Information Base for Monitoring Rural Change", ISEC, Bangalore (mimeographed), 1986.

Reddy, G R, "Patterns of Panchayati Raj in India" (Ed.), Macmillan, Madras, p. 26, 1977.

Sangita, S, "Monitoring of Rural Development Programmes, Organisational and Administrative Dimensions (Processes)", ISEC, Bangalore (mimeographed), 1986.

Shah Nawas Alam, "Economic Implications of New Agricultural Strategy in Jammu and Kashmir", (Unpublished), Deptt. of Economics, University of Kashmir.

Thimmaiah, G, "Finances of Panchayat Raj Institutions", ISEC, Bangalore (mimeographed), 1986.

Uphoff Norman and Esman J Milton, *Local Organisation for Rural Development in Asia* (unpublished report), Cornell University, New York, USA, 1974.

ELEVEN

Information Aspects Overlooked

Sreemay Basu

THE Jammu and Kashmir Panchayati Raj Bill can affect the people of the State profoundly. As Sheikh Abdullah's 'Naya Kashmir' manifesto once did, this Bill too, can elevate the level of people's involvement from reacting blindly to machinations of self-serving politicians, to responsible, active, governance of their own affairs. In this, it may well serve as a model for all other States of the Union.

For administration at any level, or for statecraft, correct anticipation of the future is a *sine qua non*. Failure to do this can spell disaster. An example of the latter may be our China Policy of the '50s, which culminated later, in the Sino-Indian war and the annexation of vast tracts of our land. As an example of the former, our Second Five-Year Plan comes to mind. The Second Plan laid down the foundation for the preservation of India's economic and industrial independence and has allowed us, in a troubled bipolar world, to follow a non-aligned path. It put us on a course in which our political and economic aspirations converged, and though drafted in the '50s, is likely to see us, without fundamental difficulties (in spite of recent policy deviations) into the 21st century. Our Constitution also has the same fundamental robustness of being able to allow for future developments.

The Jammu and Kashmir Bill too, must not only address the needs of the present but anticipate and allow for the needs of the future. This is especially necessary because the Bill is of such fundamental importance. It must lay the foundations of people's involvement in the governance of their own affairs at the grassroots level so strongly, that this power of the people cannot easily be misappropriated.

The Panchayati Raj Bill is an instrument for the devolution of power. Administrative, financial and legal procedures through which powers of governance are exercised by a polity shall rely on information. Information-gathering mechanisms are in fact built into and form an important facet of these procedures. These mechanisms, like the rules of audit for the financial and evidence for the legal procedures can be highly specific, specialised and formalised. They have evolved through practice in a sustained bid to establish the whole facts about the issue under consideration and to prevent obfuscation or distortion of the pertinent facts. The means of obtaining such information, have been mostly direct, largely manual and therefore, available to all literate people. The information revolution currently under way is changing this radically. It seems likely that the chasm between those with direct access to the new technologies and those without, will become as deep as that which now exists between the literate and the illiterate.

There are three important aspects of this issue:

1. Use of remote sensing devices for obtaining information, especially at the macro level,
2. Use of computers for both storage and processing of such information, and
3. The evolution of techniques of analysis which capitalise on the speed and power of the computers and allow insights into complex processes which are not accessible by long-hand methods.

Regarding the first aspect, most people are by now familiar with the use of satellites to produce accurate topographical maps; to track, chart and predict the weather; to measure amounts of vegetative and forest cover and amounts of crops under cultivation; and of course, for the purpose of gathering military intelligence. These require simple photographic and photogrammetric techniques. The more recent applications of remote sensing devices range from the use of nuclear magnetic resonance scans to generate images of diseased organs in a human body to thermal scans of vegetation and forest cover by satellites, to locate diseased crops or diseased trees. It is also possible now-a-days to locate and map ore deposits not only on land but even at the bottom of sea beds through satellites. This is an area of almost continuous development. Newer and more powerful sensing devices that see farther and use new mediums like sonar, electromagnetic fields and thermal traces, are used to obtain more and more information from more and more remote sources.

Regarding the second aspect, it is also now possible for such photographic, magnetic, sonic and thermal images to be automatically converted to digital form and be stored in almost instantly accessible data banks. This is another area of continuous development. Computers that process data electronically are getting faster, more reliable and cheaper all the time. An ordinary personal computer (PC) of today has as much computing power as the mainframes of the '50s — and for a minute fraction of the cost. This process is continuing with developments in large scale integration and is likely to take a quantum jump when super conductivity reaches room temperatures and is incorporated into chip technology.

A simultaneous revolution has been taking place in the form of parallel processing. This involves the use of array processors to partition and perform computations simultaneously rather than sequentially. Computing time is reduced manifold and correspondingly, the power increases in direct proportion. Already, this form of processing is available in the PC(AT) and mini computer range. It would not take an oracle to predict that the fastest supercomputers being imported by India today at a cost of crores of rupees, will be sitting as desk top models in undergraduate dormitories within 10 years, perhaps even within five.

The final revolution in this field has occurred in the way information is stored. It has been pointed out that sonic, photographic, magnetic and thermal images can be converted into digital form and stored. The usual media for such storage has been magnetic tapes and discs. Now, with the introduction of optical discs, the amount of information that can be stored in a given space without loss of integrity or coherence has again increased vastly. It is possible to accommodate entire encyclopaedias in discs the size of ordinary long-playing records.

The third aspect involves the capacity to generate, store, access and instantly manipulate phenomenal amounts of data which has also given impetus to the evolution of analytical techniques which require great computing power. Some of these techniques like modelling and simulation which are now-a-days used routinely in planning, and for policy making are reviewed briefly later.

What does this information revolution imply? Currently the US, primarily through NASA and the USSR through their Soyuz satellites have perhaps more accurately compiled and coordinated macro level data and estimates about India's (and most other countries') geography and environment, extent of development activities, defence installations, agricultural and industrial production, than we ourselves have. It is not simply a matter of gathering the data, but also of verifying, converting to comparable bases, analysing and evaluating disparate bits to form comprehensive, accurate assessments. The political leverage of having such information about other countries is obvious. It is compounded manifold if the country itself does not have independent access to such information-gathering and maintaining mechanisms. In fact, no autonomy is possible without such means. The Government of India is alive to both the possibilities and the dangers of the situation. That is why we are one of the few underdeveloped countries who have indigenously developed devices dedicated to communications and remote sensing. This is being further strengthened by the National Informatics Centres (NIC) which will connect computers at the block level with progressively larger installations at district, State, regional headquarters and a master facility with supercomputers in Delhi, through an on-line satellite-based communications system. The Rural Development Ministry has plans to set up a parallel information-gathering network through posts and telegraphs and telex lines. Such networks are necessary for the efficient acquisition and transmission of micro level data (demographic, socio-economic, landuse and revenue records etc.) which are required in addition to macro level data for analyses and planning. Such micro level data has to be generated in the 'field'. The NIC therefore, proposes to employ and post-information officers to set up procedures for the acquisition and transmission of such data. District centres are being set up all over the country and block level facilities will follow.

The situation that obtains for India in the international sphere is also valid (obviously, to a different degree) in the context of the panchayats, the States, and the Union Government. Suppose the Union Government wishes to lease land from a panchayat for purposes of 'national' development in light of information obtained through these state-of-the-art sophisticated devices. The panchayats can hardly protect their own interest in the matter if they too are not made aware of the parameters. It is not simply a matter of denial of access to information in bargaining situations, but also, of the panchayats being able to interpret, analyse and comprehend the inputs that are necessary for modern-day planning and administration.

This is particularly important in the light of re-orientation that the entire planning process in India is undergoing. Till now, it has been the usual practice to address various facets in an exercise of planning in a hierarchical fashion, rather than simultaneously. Sectoral and technical plans are usually formulated and formalised before place-oriented or spatial planning is undertaken. People-oriented planning usually comes at the very last.

This 'top-down' approach has, in some cases, led to serious misfits. Industries have been planted in places without regard for locational and space economies resulting in high production costs. Projects have been planned which displace population and disrupt entire life-styles. Customs and mores developed over millennia in symbiosis with particular habitat are overnight rendered irrelevant. Such populations may be given alternate shelter and jobs (perhaps in some of the uneconomic industries mentioned earlier) but assimilation into the economic mainstream cannot be achieved instantly and serious problems ensue. In the violence of sudden transformation, a thread from the rich fabric of our cultural diversity is lost for ever.

The Government has now recognised the need for 'bottom-up' planning to complement the centralised 'top-down' framework already in practice. The present emphasis on district level planning is evidence of this concern. District level planning is essentially an attempt to incorporate both spatial dimensions and the needs of target groups (people) in development policy.

This has major implications for both panchayats and their district level organisations. In the 'top-down' approach, the emphasis at the district level is on disbursement rather than on planning. In States which have had functioning panchayats, district plans are prepared even now, but these are largely aggregations of lists of wants compiled by the constituent panchayats. In any event, these 'plans' have had little, if any, input in the process that establishes how much funds will be available for implementation. The centralised planning that made available development funds to the panchayats (through diverse channels and agencies of both State and Central governments) and the district plans drawn up by the panchayats themselves, were separate evolutionary entities. The panchayats therefore, had little incentive to make their plans practical, to undertake the objective analysis required to ensure that 'needs' replaced 'wants', to undertake detailed studies to prioritise these needs optimally, to consider macro parameters to ensure that their own panchayat needs were viable in both district and national contexts, and to undertake the several iterations required to transform plans based on local optima to absolute (national) ones.

In the newly revised scenario as the Government of India now proceeds through enactment to establish a direct linkage between district, State and national planning and their implementation process, the panchayats can seize the opportunity for effective participation in the planning and implementation of schemes for their own development. For this, they will have to take upon themselves the responsibility to undertake all that is required for modern-day planning and administration. Otherwise, decentralisation will be in name only.

These then, are two information-related issues the Panchayati Raj Bill has to address:

1. The mechanisms and constitutional guarantees which can enable access of local government at grass roots levels to information without censure. Not that one wishes to impute other motives, however, it is inherent in the nature of centralised bureaucracies to limit access to information, often to ludicrous degrees. Till a prohibitory agreement was signed, it was easier to obtain accurate thematic maps of any part of India from NASA (for $ 20) than to obtain such maps from the Union Government. And this is by no means peculiar to the Indian context. Even in the US, Universities have sometimes forced federal authorities to de-classify data under threat of obtaining the same information from agencies like Soyuzkarta in the USSR. The NIC and the other networks being set up at enormous cost to the people of India should not be allowed to deteriorate into one-way channels to acquire and centralise data but must also be nurtured as conduits for dissemination and access to the information pool. This will require formalised interaction of panchayats with State government mechanisms and personnel, as well as

Central Government ones, particularly, the block level installations and the information officers. Formalised interaction means defining spheres of responsibility of the various agencies and their accountability *inter se* in detail, through enactment.

2. The panchayats have also to be provided with the technical expertise necessary for the use of such information channels and information. Just as it is necessary for them to undergo training for conducting adalats or for maintaining accounts, it is necessary for them to be acquainted with the workings of such information channels and then to be provided with personnel capable of obtaining data of interest to the panchayats and of doing the necessary analyses. It is not enough to provide them with interpreted data. They have to acquire the wherewithal for doing their own interpretation. In a sense this information technology business is more difficult than legal, administrative or fiscal matters. It is possible to be illiterate, but have an innate Solomon-like sense of natural justice. Spending within one's means, the fundamental principle of financial management, is not a difficult concept to clarify. But computers, satellites and mathematical models are not easily understood in everyday village terms. Special efforts and provisions will be necessary for the future.

The logic access to information at the panchayat level is implicit in the *raison d'etre* of the Panchayat Bill itself. Unless, the panchayats themselves have direct control over the sources of information of all kinds — their dependence on a centralised agency is liable to be manipulated in a manner not necessarily conducive to the interest of, or in conformity with, the will of the people. Whether in the words of J. S. Mill (Good government is no substitute for self-government), or in the formulations of pluralism by Laski, or in the concept of a classless society envisaged by Marx, accumulated human wisdom has inexorably pointed out that there is no alternative to autonomous participation of people at grass roots levels. Devolution of power, as completely as possible, may be the only process by which qualitative changes can be brought about and which people can evolve in our own rural hinterland.

True, the mechanics of devolution of power is a complex thing. Since Montesquieu's idea of separation of powers, innumerable experiments of checks and balances have been made in statecraft at various levels. Even the concept of federalism to balance the interest of the States and the Centre, has not been easy to translate in concrete terms. Australia, Canada, USA and others have tried to solve the problem in their own way. The problems in our country called for a Sarkaria Commission to help in the resolution. But whatever the difficulties, there is no escape from renewing the endeavour for which we can define the goal. We have the accumulated experience of the past to benefit from.

The present state of use of computers for planning in Europe and America is that of extensive use of modelling for more and more diverse applications, particularly for simulation of alternate scenarios in response to planned interventions. The outcome of such simulation exercises are considered for policy formulation and also for development of strategies for implementation. These models for 'description' and 'prediction' can be exceedingly complex comprising various partial sub-models as building blocks. They have to be 'dynamic', allowing relationships between variables to change over time, as indeed they will in reality. The degrees of complexity demand very large computing capacity and extensive computational time. Moreover, large data-sets are necessary especially for dynamic models which require time-series data (and primary data of good quality is always very very expensive to obtain). In spite of all the effort, some planners find such models absurdly simplistic and incapable of representing the real world in any real sense. (This feeling stems largely from the experience of the 1960s when land-use and transportation 'modelling' first began. The modellers promised all and achieved little. Their formulations were impractical and over-ambitious especially, since the available computing power was very limited. In general, they met the fate of all things overweight and underpowered — oblivion. Modelling currently, however, uses a different approach altogether. The new generation models utilise the vastly increased computing power now available in attractive, user-friendly software packages which are designed to perform a limited set of specific analytical tasks. This 'core' is then added to overtime and the package acquires more and more power — the ability to do additional tasks, and each task in a choice of different ways).

An alternative view is that precisely because of the complexities of the real world, a model (which is really a working description) including important factors and their interactions, is an absolute necessity as a frame within which to tackle any problem of planning. In the absence of such a framework all planning is *ad hoc* and will inevitably result in consequences that are unforeseen.

Another advantage of a 'description' of this sort is that it makes assumptions explicit, allowing other planners (other than the authors) to refine the 'description' should some assumptions have lost validity overtime; and to add or subtract to the basic fomulation without loss of coherence. In short, it removes plans to a large degree from the realm of personal and artistic arbitrariness. Models rationalise planning and allow development continuity.

The simplification of reality that modelling entails is also perhaps the only means of making complex real-life problems tractable. Consider a map (which is also a description of reality), even a pocket map of the city of Delhi; because it simplifies all the maze of streets and buildings and open greens and the topography into a few lines, it fits in the pocket and can be used by a tourist to get around. No doubt a map on the scale of 1:1 would be able to capture the 'reality' of Delhi in all detail, but it would require all of Delhi to spread the map on, and would hardly be useful as a guide for the tourist.

There is another reason why models are of vital importance to planning. A project architect or engineer is able to appreciate the consequences of his decisions as soon as the construction is completed. He can use the feedback to modify his future designs. A planner, on the other hand, may not even witness the full consequence of his decisions in a lifetime. Urban settlements and regions planned by him may require more than a lifetime to mature. The impact of an urban or regional level plan is so pervasive and extensive that this sort of a lag is inevitable before the system has time to stabilise. In this scale, models help in the exploration of a range of possible consequences through simulation. Simulation aids planners' understanding and leads to the reformulation of problems and their solutions. (In view of its importance, it seems essential, that such modelling and simulation initiated for all levels of policy making and planning in India forthwith. Past constraints have, of course, included lack of basic computing facilities but this is now being removed. The further requirements are for software, data-bases and trained personnel. For a vast and diverse country like India, building data-base have to be cooperative ventures. Organisation is required to initiate mechanisms by which this could be done. The tasks would be: first, to coordinate the acquisition and development of software; second, to obtain funds, sponsor and coordinate the development of databases to ensure both quality and portability so that data acquired by one institution can be shared by all; and third, to organise courses and training for professionals, technicians and other users. The final task, of course, is to demonstrate how such data and analyses can be used by private and public planning bodies to influence policy decisions).

And now to the future. The future lies in the linking of the models and simulation capabilities of the programme developed by planners to the 'computer imaging' capabilities developed by researchers in computer graphics. The state-of-the-art is such that Cornell University which is at the forefront of this development, expects with the help of parallel processing to generate images fast enough to simulate 'walking through hypothetical space in real time'.

What does this mean? It means computers will be able to generate wholly synthetic video films of wholly imaginary urban settlements (or villages, regions, eco-systems, biosphere reserves etc.) complete with simulated buildings, simulated people, simulated traffic of all kinds, even simulated traffic accidents at badly designed street intersections and visually display the simulated growth, decay and trnsformation of these proposed cities and regions in consonance with future 'scenarios' of development. Or, it could evaluate the consequences of an intervention in an existing urban area (or village, region, etc.), say a new building at Connaught Place, and demonstrate its impact on the image (from any viewpoint), its effect on traffic and the transportation networks, on the adjoining buildings in physical terms, shadows, energy dispersion, effect on shopping, revenue base — in short, on any aspect of interest to planners, even before sanctions are applied for.

When is this future possible? By the year 2000? No, within five years at most. To dispel scepticism, an excerpt of a report in *Time* news magazine on the First World Supercomputer Exhibition held in Santa Clara, California in May 1987, follows:

> "Computer-generated images are now vital laboratory tools"
>
> Among the flashy hardware and software on display at last week's First World Supercomputer Exhibition in Santa Clara, California, the small Cornell National Supercomputer Facility booth attracted attention out of proportion to its size. There on a large video screen, more than a thousand stars wheeled

around a newly formed black hole, an incredibly dense, bizarre entity with gravity so strong that not even light can escape from it. As nearby stars were sucked in by its gravity, the hole grew. By the time the system stabilised, nearly half its stars were gone. Conventioneers were fascinated.

But not as much as some scientists were. Before their equations were converted into computer images, astrophysicists had predicted that only a tenth as many stars in such a system would be eaten by a black hole. This was no isolated case. Across the nation, in disciplines ranging from geophysics to medicine to entomology, scientists are discovering that computer images can sometimes lead to a better understanding of nature. Borrowing a leaf from Hollywood's special-effects book (and in some cases hiring Hollywood technicians), they are converting their data into video form. Because the human brain is exquisitely adept at picking up visual cues, scientists have begun benefiting from what Robert Langridge of the University of California at San Francisco calls 'computer-aided insights'. Says Langridge, who uses 3-D graphics to model biological molecules: 'Computer graphics gives us a window into what is going on, rather than just a scientific result. It has become an experimental tool'.

TWELVE

West Bengal's Lessons for Jammu and Kashmir

Arun Ghosh

THE Jammu and Kashmir Panchayati Raj Bill, 1988, promises to usher in a new era in the history of the State. This brief narration of the West Bengal experience in the matter of planning at the block and district levels since 1985-86, is presented here in the hope that the lessons of the West Bengal experience would be of benefit to all those who are concerned with the experiment in Jammu and Kashmir.

Problems of Coordination

As the outset, it may be stated that the local panchayats in West Bengal—at the gram panchayat (equivalent to the halqa panchayat of J & K) and panchayat samiti (at the block level) – had the benefit of some years' experience at other forms of mobilisation of effort and exercise of authority, before the introduction of local level planning. The first panchayati elections (under the Left Front government) were held early in 1978, with a second one in early 1983. (A third one was held in April 1988.) Over the seven years from 1978 until the initiation of local level planning, the panchayats had been slowly inducted into diverse types of activities. The most crucial among these was the direct participation of the newly elected panchayats in the process of land reform—through identification of ceiling surplus agricultural land, identification of the landless agricultural labourers who might be the beneficiaries of any scheme of redistribution of ceiling surplus vested land, as well as identification of share croppers to be registered under 'Operation Barga'. Later, after 1980-81, the panchayats were also given the responsibility of identifying the beneficiaries of the Integrated Rural Development Programme (IRDP), as well as of the preparation and implementation of rural works programmes and schemes under the National Rural Employment Programme (NREP) and the Rural Landless Employment Guarantee Programme (RLEGP). The last two activities may, in a sense, be deemed to be a prelude to local level planning. While the identification of the specific needs (and the schemes designed to meet these needs) was initiated by the gram panchayats, the technical parameters and other details (including the requirements of funds) were prepared by the panchayat samitis which were assisted in this task by sub-assistant engineers (SAEs) who helped to prepare blueprints and supervised the implementation of schemes under the NREP and RLEGP. The mobilisation of the labour required for the purpose was the responsibility of gram panchayats at the village cluster level. For small NREP schemes, mostly concerned earlier with rural road schemes of small value, the gram panchayats had been the final authority both for approval and implementation. For large NREP and RLEGP schemes, the panchayat samitis were the final authorities both in regard to the schemes proposed and their implementation. During 1982-83, the Drought Relief Programme also provided substantial funds to a few districts, where the zilla parishads (at the district level) got into the act of devising minor irrigation and other schemes, to be implemented, again, in the same manner as diverse road building and other schemes, by the panchayat samitis and the gram panchayats, under the direction of the zilla parishads. The West Bengal government also provided some funds, to be divided among all gram panchayats, panchayat samitis and zilla parishads, for meeting their administrative expenses, with any surplus to be used for community welfare schemes. (In practice, there was no surplus left for the latter purpose under this head.)

Thus, in a sense, the panchayats at the grassroot level in West Bengal were already attuned to preparing small schemes for local development and taking action for implementing them, before the introduction of the concept of district planning with effect from

1985-86.

The need for local level planning was acutely felt in West Bengal for several reasons. (As would emerge from what follows, this is likely to be true of all States, as well as at the Centre, because of the very nature of functioning of government). First, even with the best intentions and efforts, at coordination, at the field level, the activities of different economic departments of the State government remained somewhat desparate and uncoordinated. The principle of "single line of command" recommended by the World Bank, and accepted by the Government of India in respect of all developmental schemes, which have essentially been proposed and implemented by different departments—meant that departmental representatives in the field took their instructions from and reported to only their respective officers at the headquarters (in the case of West Bengal, at Calcutta). There was, therefore, no coordination of effort between different departmental authorities at the local level and frequently, not even adequate information (in the field) as to what was being planned by the different line departments of the State government.

Second, the representation of the different line departments obviously got thinly spread. With a 1981 population of some 55 million in 341 blocks (some of them not operational) in West Bengal, on an average each block had a population of more than 1.6 lakh. Obviously, the representatives of different line departments—some only at the district level, some going down to the block level—could not reach out to the bulk of the population. As a result, the development effort of most economic departments tended to be concentrated in and around the block headquarters and did not go much further. There was in any case no coordination between the development efforts of the State government and the schemes drawn up by the panchayat bodies at the local level, under the IRDP, NREP, RLEGP and other programmes.

Finally, the efforts at the State level did not, in fact understandably could not, take note of the most pressing of local needs. For example, parts of the districts of Burdwan, Hooghly and Howrah have been in dire need of better drainage, arising partly out of the otherwise beneficial irrigation programme of the DVC canal system, but the specific needs of a few areas got swamped by the directly opposite needs of other areas. It was increasingly obvious that the wisdom and experience of officers at the State level were not enough, and that the perceptions of the people in regard to their most urgently felt needs could be given cognizance only by giving them both the authority and the responsibility, as well as the financial resources, to prepare their own plans and schemes of local development. Paramount in this approach was the concept of combining "area planning" with beneficiary oriented planning, the latter specifically with reference to the weaker sections of the population, to be assisted through the redistribution of ceiling surplus vested land, follow up support to the beneficiaries and to share croppers (registered under 'Operation Barga') by way of credit and other inputs required for farming operations, as well as through programmes like the IRDP. Such an approach could be made possible only by inducting the local panchayats in the task of 'planning' for their constituents, by combining the "area approach" with the "beneficiary-oriented approach".

Integrating the Planning Process

The formulation of district plans for 1985-86 in West Bengal was preceded by intensive preparations during the previous year. While the organisational framework would be indicated later, briefly it may be noted here that planning committees were constituted at the district and the block level (by an order of the State government), under the *sabhadhipati* (or chairman) of the zilla parishad and the *sabhapati* (or president) of the panchayat samiti, respectively. (No 'planning body' was constituted at the gram panchayat level (equivalent to the halqa panchayat in the J & K), though the latter were intimately involved in the process of preparation of block level plans, and later in implementing them). To get back to the formulation of district plans, members of the State Planning Board (and experts assisting the Board) visited most district headquarters and quite a few block headquarters, and meetings were also organised at the State headquarters (at Calcutta), wherein the local panchayat functionaries had detailed discussions in regard to the procedure to be adopted. The first task was the preparation, at the gram panchayat level, of a statement of the felt needs of the people in each village cluster, and their listing in order of priorities. These were to be collated at the block level where schemes were to be formulated with the help of the SAEs for meeting these "felt needs". The task of coordination commenced immediately thereafter. For instance, schemes for new roads were put together and after discussion between the block and gram panchayat authorities, necessary changes in alignments made so as to ensure a meaningful network of communications system. (The same procedure was repeated at a later stage, at the zilla parishad level, so that the investments on the construction of new roads could become more useful even at the village cluster level.) Or again, if any scheme for animal husbandry development was proposed at the village cluster level, they were advised to combine a scheme for increased production of fodder (and other animal feed) and to ensure the availability of the required quantity of animal feed. This was particularly important where beneficiaries of IRDP or other programmes were to be assisted to acquire high milk yielding breeds of cattle whose requirement of fodder is also significantly higher. Coordination was also necessary between the programme of land redistribution and the supply of agricultural inputs, in particular, credit, to the beneficiaries.

At the block level, an attempt was to be made to dovetail all schemes proposed at the gram panchayat level into a framework of budgetary allocations, and in particular, under the extant State level (departmental) programmes where possible, or at least classified under the relevant budgetary heads. This called for coordination between the departmental representatives at the block level (and later, at the district level) and the officials responsible for the preparation of local level plans.

To give an example of the coordination required, for instance, if the State animal husbandry department had plans to incur developmental outlay in any block, they were to be asked to consider incorporating the local felt needs (and schemes) for animal husbandry development in the departmental programme, so that (a) duplication could be avoided, and (b) maximum funding could be ensured for meeting the felt needs of the people. Or again, to reiterate what has been hinted at earlier, the programme of the State department of agriculture had to be coordinated with that of the department of animal husbandry, and of both with that of the department of cooperation (for credit supply), and so on.

A matrix of outlays necessary to implement the schemes at the block level, together with the possibility of funding was to be prepared. It may be added at this juncture that most of the schemes proposed at the village cluster level happen to be labour intensive and therefore capable of being financed under the NREP, RLEGP, the Drought Relief Programme and similar programmes on which significant sums are being spent today without any long lasting benefits by way of the build-up of capital assets in rural areas. Most small irrigation and road construction schemes require a large element of labour. Indeed, even brick-paved roads can be made predominantly labour intensive by combining brickmaking with road making as an integrated scheme, the labour component of the total outlay thereby meeting the minimum percentage requirements prescribed under NREP/RLEGP. In any case, with the low level of employment and incomes for large sections of the rural population in most parts of West Bengal, the accent in the preparation of schemes at the village cluster and block level was to be on labour intensive schemes, thereby making NREP/RLEGP funds a major source for financing local level plans.

The process of local level planning thus succeeded in, so to say, killing three birds with one stone: first, providing employment to rural labour which is the primary objective of these anti-poverty programmes; second, building capital assets in rural areas with the available funds; and finally, successfully meeting the most urgent needs and aspirations of the people. For example, it was found that many gram panchayats wanted to have school buildings or extensions thereof for existing primary schools (for children) which were not functioning effectively because of the absence of *pucca* buildings; and quite a few of the gram panchayats attached high priority to the construction of school buildings or their extension. These schemes could not be proposed earlier under NREP/RLEGP because their cost was obviously more than the available funds, and also did not meet the labour component criterion. With the availability of State funds under a new budgetary head entitled 'district plan schemes' given to district planning authorities, the construction of school buildings was given a high priority by many gram panchayats.

The dovetailing of schemes under NREP/RLEGP and similar programmes within the framework of local level plans was thus a major objective of the exercise undertaken, where necessary, even by quickly amending or modifying the schemes proposed earlier on which action was yet to commence. [In retrospect, this was easily possible for NREP, which was within the authority of the State government to approve. In respect of RLEGP, where all schemes (down to small, village level schemes) require the prior approval of the Central Government, difficulties arose during 1985-86 because of the unwarranted refusal of the Central authorities to allow any substitution of new schemes for schemes approved earlier. In the event, the dovetailing of RLEGP outlays within the district plan had to be deferred during 1985-86, for subsequent plan years.]

A brief illustration of the matrix of outlays proposed may clarify the manner in which block level plans were to be finally summarised.

Department/ Head of Account	Outlay proposed and proposed source of funding			
	Depart-mental outlay of State government	NREP/ RLEGP/ Drought Relief Program-me etc.	Dis-trict plan schemes fund (from State Govt.)	Other sour-ce of fun-ding (to be mentioned)
1. **Agriculture**				
1.1 Crop husbandry				
1.1.1 Supply of minikits of seeds and fertilisers				
1.1.2 Seed multiplication				
1.2. Soil conservation				
1.2.1. Contour bunding in deforested, degraded area				
2. **Irrigation**				
2.1 Minor irrigation				
2.1.1 Sinking of shallow tubewells				
2.1.3 Excavation/enlargement of ponds				

The above is a small (and partial cross-section of the schematic) summary presentation of the block level plans. Behind each figure, under each head of account, there was a collection of schemes with full details in the overall block plan document. There were to be two such summaries: one giving the *desired* pattern and the other based on actuals (especially in regard to departmental and other "outside" funds), the only resource totally under the command of the local authorities being the District Plan Scheme fund made available by the State government (and to an extent, funds released under the NREP).

Incidentally, one advantage of the above effort was that *information* on the extant schemes of different authorities under implementation got collated and known to the block and district level authorities for the first time.

This information was not available at one place even in the State headquarters. Thus the mere collation of the information on the actual pattern of developmental outlay being incurred in the field showed up the gaps, duplication and the inappropriate focus on relatively low priority projects by departmental authorities in certain instances. The information collected became a valuable input for planning by the local authorities who could then draw up schemes to meet those needs which did not figure in the departmental plans, or which would act as complements to departmental plans.

The information was also useful for revamping and reorienting departmental plans, in the next round, so as to be more useful to the populace covered by the diverse programmes.

To recapitulate, the "needs statements" of village clusters were collated by the gram panchayats, and schemes were drawn up by the panchayat authorities at the block level to meet these "needs". The task of drawing up schemes was thus basically left to the panchayat samitis at the block level, though the implementation of the schemes finally approved remained the responsibility of the gram panchayats at the village cluster (or *anchal*) level. The final approval of the plans drawn up by the panchayat samitis had, however, to come from the district level planning authorities, partly because the sum total of funds required for all block level plans exceeded the resources available, and partly because of the need for greater coordination between diverse block level plans at a higher level. However, the plans prepared at the block level required to be pruned at the district level, and this has remained to this day a matter of some controversy and debate. The approval procedure in West Bengal therefore needs to be explained separately, for therein arose certain problems.

Approval of Procedure

The West Bengal government had by a notification constituted the following machinery for local level planning:

a. Block planning committee, the members being the pradhans of all gram panchayats, *plus* departmental representatives at the block level, presided over by the sabhapati of the panchayat samiti, with the block development officer (BDO) acting as the secretary of the committee;
b. District planning committee, the members being the sabhapatis of all panchayat samitis, *plus* senior departmental representatives in the district, *plus* the karmadhyakshas of the zilla parishad, *plus* MLAs and MPs from the district, presided over by the sabhadhipati of the zilla parishad, and the district magistrate acting as the secretary-cum-chief executive officer and
c. District planning and development council, consisting of the district planning committee, *plus* the chairman of all municipalities in the district, *plus* the heads of any other governmental area authorities in the district, presided over by a minister of the West Bengal government coming from the district.

The addition of MLAs and MPs in the district planning committee was a compromise; these functionaries felt left out when the initial proposal did not include them in the district planning committee. Also, at the initial stage, the sabhadhipati of the zilla parishad was to be given the final authority of planning for the district. But West Bengal has a large number of municipalities and notified area authorities, and again, as a compromise, a superior body — the district planning and coordination committee (DPCC) — was constituted, with a State government minister as the chairman, this body being given the final authority to approve the district plans drawn up by the district planning committee. Incidentally, prior to the introduction of district planning, West Bengal had a system of district level coordination committees (DLCC) in each district, presided over by a minister of the State government, mainly for ensuring coordination of work, especially in the matter of land reform, land distribution, IRDP, RLEGP, NREP, etc. With the constitution of the DPCC, the DLCC became redundant, and its functions were subsumed in the DPCC. Thus, one justification for constituting the DPCC as an approval body above the DPC was the existence of the DLCC, with the responsibility of coordinating the work of departmental authorities with that of the panchayati bodies.

Thus, the district plan had to be approved by the DPCC, and only then became operational. The implementation of the plan, however, was left to the district planning committee, the block planning committee, the municipalities (wherever relevant) and the gram panchayats. In general, contractors were to be avoided for all works programmes, the use of unemployed labour thus becoming mandatory involving the participation of the gram panchayats for the mobilisation of labour for all rural works. (The same applied for municipalities in principle, but in fact, the system did not work smoothly in urban areas.) The block planning committees and the district planning committees were to be assisted by the sanction of staff (mainly SAEs and accounts clerks at the block level, and both junior engineers and technical experts like agronomists, economists and groundwater experts at the district level). Thus, both planning and implementation (of rural programmes) became the responsibility of the panchayats, but the approval of the plans was left to a higher body presided over by a minister of the State government.

Political and Bureaucratic Problems

The first problem arose with MLAs and MPs being made members of the district planning committees. These functionaries, living in metropolitan areas may, in general, be said to be somewhat out of touch with the day-to-day problems and needs of people in remote villages. In any case, their major preoccupations and therefore their perceptions are by and large somewhat different from those of people at the village cluster level. The MLAs and MPs have, over the years, become "power brokers" — and for local level planning one needs a different view. The insistence of MLAs and MPs to be made members of the district planning committee appeared to stem from the danger they perceived in the development of a new centre of power, of the growth of influence and prestige of a new set of local leaders. They felt left out and they obviously wanted to have share of what they perceived as new "patronage", in terms of funds available for developmental outlay, now devolving on district and block planning committees. This is clearly one of the problems to be carefully tackled, namely, the increasing involvement of "outsiders" in the process of local level planning.

Indeed, if one were to go back in time and examine the history of district planning in Maharashtra, one perceives the danger to genuine local level planning from this development. During the '60s, Maharashtra embarked upon the process of district planning by the newly elected zilla parishads; and the experiment was so successful in enthusing the local populace that not only the MLAs and MPs but also the then State government in Maharashtra grew suspicious of the development of a new power centre at the district level. Hence, gradually, the authority of the panchayats was clipped, the process of district planning converted to planning on paper (by the people's representatives) with the district magistrate being given the final authority to prepare the district plans, and the district magistrate in turn took his orders from the State headquarters. The panchayats were relegated to the position of implementing whatever plans were drawn up at the dictates of the State government. Much the same thing has happened in Gujarat also, which took up district planning through the panchayats around the same time as Maharashtra.

In West Bengal, this problem has not surfaced in the same manner yet, but in certain districts, the quality of the district plan has suffered because of the interference of influential MLAs and MPs. One has to realise in this context that the concept of decentralised planning involves getting the perceptions of the local populace reflected in the plans drawn up for their benefit. The plans must be drawn up by them and not merely for them. The process of Central (as well as State level) planning has hitherto followed the system of planning by experts, generally located far away from where the action is, doubtless in the name of the people and in the guise of the 'public interest'. Planning so far has remained *for* the people, *not by* them. Herein arises a major difference in perceptions. The people, the common people, generally know what is good for them, better than outside experts. They (the people) may need technical advice and guidance, but they must exercise their judgement to decide on the manner of advancing their own welfare. This way, the local level plans would not only be of direct benefit to them, the people would also acquire greater confidence and self-reliance, and thereby free themselves of the shackles of centuries of docility and passive acceptance of the dictates of outsiders.

Hence, the procedure in West Bengal, of having a cabinet minister of the State government preside over the district planning and coordination committee is also a compromise which is best avoided. In Karnataka, not only has the present government avoided this but has taken the additional step of conferring on the president of the

per capita terms, next only to Nagaland, it would only require the necessary political determination and commitment to allocate part of the available resources and possibly also delegate part of the responsibility for some selected economic activities, to the panchayat bodies. The district could be made a focal centre of such delegated authority and financial powers.

Perhaps, in addition to the above basic problems which emerge from the West Bengal experience at panchayati raj, one essential feature of the West Bengal system needs to be highlighted. From an early stage, the panchayat authorities in West Bengal have been required to give wide publicity to all decisions taken by the panchayats. Thus, for example, in the case of IRDP, or land redistribution, the names of beneficiaries and the precise assistance recommended are required to be displayed on the notice board of the gram panchayat. Similar publicity is to be given to all decisions taken in regard to schemes approved, the list of beneficiaries (where relevant), and other particulars. This has been a salutary feature of the functioning of the panchayats, and has proved to be an effective check on arbitrary decisions. "Openness" of all decisions taken by the panchayats is thus ensured, and the possibility of favouritism or graft minimised. Even though not all villagers are literate, and even though not all villagers can (or do) read the notices put up, the very fact of their publicity, and the awareness and interest of rival parties and interest groups provide the assurance that such publicity is not in vain, and is a check on arbitrary decisions being taken by the pradhans of the gram panchayats wherein all decisions can get discussed. Thus, "openness" and wide publicity to all decisions of the panchayat authorities (in Jammu and Kashmir, at the halqa and block levels) could help to foster greater awareness, participation, and eventual success of the experiment.

The other lesson from the West Bengal experience is that the panchayats are in the best position to plan not only for the development of the infrastructure and the removal of infrastructural weaknesses in each area, but also for increasing the *capacity* of the people to become viable, through the integration of programmes of education, health and other social services. For example, the provision of wholesome but simple mid-day meals to school children not only ensures attendance in primary schools but also helps to improve the health of the children. And such programmes are easier for local (panchayat) authorities to run than for a distant State government to administer through the bureaucratic apparatus. Thus, given the proper guidance and guidelines, and the required financial support, the panchayats are in the best position to *plan* for local development.

Local Bodies Must have Financial Powers

The above is an extremely brief narration of the procedure adopted for decentralised planning in West Bengal, in the hope that the lessons of the West Bengal experience would be of some use in introducing decentralised planning through panchayati raj bodies in Jammu and Kashmir. It may be added that the success of the experiment in West Bengal stems essentially from the process of politicisation of the panchayat elections—indeed, the politicisation of the entire countryside through the political activities of the CPI-M and other leftist parties in the rural areas—and the impetus and experience imparted to the local panchayats by making them the focal points of important decision-making tasks in connection with land reform and the implementation of rural anti-poverty programmes like the IRDP, NREP and RLEGP. These latter functions could similarly be entrusted to the panchayats in Jammu and Kashmir in any case, command over these would immediately provide a basis, and a minimum of resources, for planning and implementing, at the halqa level, schemes for the benefit of the local communities, as well as for the uplift of the weaker sections of the populace. The awakening of the awareness of the people and giving them a sense of pride and of authority over their own destiny can be facilitated by giving the panchayats both the responsibility and the financial powers in regard to diverse social and economic services. That has been the experience in West Bengal, where the panchayats have readily responded to the task of planning at the district and block level.

The West Bengal experience also indicates some problems that could arise in the process. The first of these problems arise from the fact that power is not willingly shed by anybody. That applies both to politicians and to bureaucrats. It would therefore require both vision and sagacity to contain the *internal* struggles within government, and to hand over the required powers and authority to panchayat bodies. One fact of life is that power tends to veer to those who control the purse. Adequate devolution of financial powers to the panchayat bodies would thus be a major factor in giving them status and responsibility as well as in securing the cooperation of officialdom.

Finally, there is a tendency in elitist circles to discount the wisdom of the people. The West Bengal experience has demonstrated that in practice some of the district plans drawn up by people without any previous experience at planning are better in content and more consistent and coordinated than the State level plan or even the all-India plan framework drawn up by a large body of professionals and experts in the Planning Commission. The people, it may be stressed, know what is good for them. They may need the guidance and advice on technical matters (as for instance, the technical specifications of the bridge), but they are in a better position to accord priorities to diverse alternatives than planners and experts from outside. It is, therefore, possible to entrust greater responsibilities to the elected panchayat bodies even where one may think that these newly elected bodies may not really know what is good for them. That, in brief, is the most important lesson of the experience of panchayati raj in both Karnataka and West Bengal.

Annexure I

THE JAMMU AND KASHMIR PANCHYATI RAJ ACT, 1989.

WHEREAS it is expedient to promote and develop Panchayati Raj in the State as an instrument of vigorous Local Self Government to secure the effective participation of the people in the decision making process and for over-seeing implementation of developmental programmes.

CHAPTER I

PRELIMINARY

1. *Short title, extent and commencement* — (1) This Act may be called the Jammu and Kashmir Panchayati Raj Act, 1989.

(2) It extends to the whole of the State of Jammu and Kashmir.

(3) It shall come into force on such date as the Government may, by notification in the Government Gazette, appoint in this behalf.

2. *Definitions* — (1) In this Act, unless the context otherwise requires, —

(a) "Block" means the area comprising such contiguous number of Halqas as may be determined by the Government from time to time;

(b) "Block Development Council" means Block Development Council constituted under section 27 of this Act;

(c) "Building" includes any shop, house, hut, out-house, shed, stable, super-structure and land appertinent to a building whether used for the purpose of human habitation or otherwise and whether of masonry, bricks, wood, mud, thatch, metal or any other material whatever, and includes a wall and a wall but does not include mud-wall built round agricultural land not abutting on the public road;

(d) "Case" means a criminal proceeding in respect of an offence triable by a Halqa Panchayati Adalat;

(e) "Chairman" means the Chairman of —

(i) the Panchayati Adalat;
(ii) the Block Development Council;
(iii) the District Planning and Development Board;

(f) "Constituency" means a ward for which a member is to be or has been elected;

(g) "District Planning and Development Board" means a District Planning and Development Board constituted under this Act;

(h) "Election Authority" means Chief Electoral Officer of the State;

(i) "Electoral Roll" means the rolls as may be prepared in accordance with the provisions of this Act;

(j) "Halqa" means the area comprising a village or such continguous number of villages as may be determined by the Government from time to time:

Provided that the Halqas shall be determined in such a manner that the population of any Halqa does not exceed 3,000 in the hilly areas and 4,500 in the plain areas;

Provided further that the unit of a village shall not be disturbed.

(k) "Halqa Panchayat" means a Halqa Panchayat constituted under section 4 of this Act;

(l) "Naib-Sarpanch" means the Naib-Sarpanch of the Halqa Panchayat;

(m) "Panch" means a member of Halqa Panchayat whether elected or nominated under this Act;

(n) "Panchayati Adalat" means a Panchayati Adalat constituted under section 47 of this Act for the purpose of trial of suits and cases;

(o) "Prescribed" means prescribed by rules made under this Act;

(p) "Prescribed Authority" means such authority as may be appointed by the Government by notification, for all or any of the provisions of this Act;

(q) "Rules" means the rules made under this Act;

(r) "Sarpanch" means the Sarpanch of the Halqa Panchayat;

(s) "Schedule" means the Schedule appended to this Act;

(t) "Suit" means a civil suit;

(u) "Vice-Chairman" means the Vice-Chairman of —

(i) the Block Development Council;

(ii) the District Planning and Development Board.

(v) "Village" means a parcel or parcels of land having a separate name and known limits in the revenue records and not included in the limits of a Municipality, Cantonment or Town Area Committee or Notified Area Committee.

(2) In this Act, the expressions "decree", "decree holder", "judgement-debtor", "Legal representative" and "movable property" shall have the same meaning as is assigned to them in the Code of Civil Procedure, Samvat 1977.

3. *Act to over-ride other laws* — The provisions of this Act shall have effect notwithstanding anything inconsistent therewith contained in any other law for the time being in force or instrument having effect by virtue of any such law.

CHAPTER II

HALQA PANCHAYAT

4. *Establishment and constitution of Halqa Panchayat* — (1) There shall be a Halqa Panchayat for every Halqa.

(2) Every Halqa Panchayat shall bear the name of the place where it is headquarted.

(3) Every Halqa Panchayat shall consist of such number of Panchs not less than seven and not more than eleven, including the Sarpanch, as the prescribed authority may, from time to time, fix in this behalf:

Provided that if the prescribed authority is satisfied that women or Scheduled Castes or any other class are not represented in the

9. *Supersession of Halqa Panchayat* — (1) If in the opinion of the Government a Halqa Panchayat is incompetent to perform or persistently makes default in the performance of duties imposed on it by or under this Act, the Government may, by notification, supersede such Halqa Panchayat:

Provided that no order under this section shall be passed unless the Halqa Panchayat is called upon to show cause why such an order shall not be passed.

(2) The period of supersession shall not exceed six months during which the elections shall be held.

(3) When an order under sub-section (1) is passed, the Government may, by order in writing, make arrangements for carrying out the work of the Halqa Panchayat for such period as it may specify, but not exceeding six months.

(4) If a Halqa Panchayat is superseded —

(i) the Sarpanch and Panchs of the Halqa Panchayat shall, from the date of the notification, vacate their office;

(ii) the funds and other property vested in the Halqa Panchayat shall, during the period of supersession, vest in the person/body entrusted with the function under sub-section (3).

10. *Remuneration to Sarpanch and Panchs* — (1) Every Sarpanch shall be entitled to such monthly honorarium as may be specified by the Government.

(2) Each Panch shall be entitled to such sitting fee as may be specified by the Government.

11. *Resignation* — A Sarpanch, Naib-Sarpanch, a Panch of a Halqa Panchayat may, by writing under his hand, addressed to such authority as may be prescribed, resign his office and his office shall thereupon become vacant.

CHAPTER III

POWERS AND FUNCTIONS

12. *Powers and functions* — (1) Subject to the provisions of this Act, it shall be the duty of each Halqa Panchayat to make provision for the following subject to availability of funds at its disposal:

(i) to prepare plans for the development of the halqa;

(ii) to undertake measures for the implementation of the developmental plans;

(iii) to specifically deal with problems of soil conservation, water management, social forestry, rural industrialisation, agriculture, sheep and animal husbandry, sanitation, health and other welfare programmes;

(iv) regulations of buildings, shops and entertainment houses and checking of offensive or dangerous trades;

(v) construction and maintenance of slaughter houses, regulation of sale and preservation of meat and processing of skins and hides;

(vi) regulation of sale and preservation of fish, vegetables and other perishable articles and food;

(vii) regulation of fairs and festivals;

(viii) preparation and implementation of special development plans for alleviating poverty and employment generation through and besides programme, like Integrated Rural Development Programme, National Rural Employment Programme, Rural Landless Employment Guarantee Programme and Housing for Scheduled Castes and Backward Classes;

(ix) all matters involving regulation, supervision, maintenance and support, incidental to, or necessary for the more efficient discharge of the above functions and those which may be entrusted to Halqa Panchayat under the provisions of the Act.

(2) The Halqa Panchayat shall be involved in the implementation of scheme of universalisation of elementary education and other educational programmes.

(3) The Halqa Panchayat shall also perform such other functions and duties as may be assigned or entrusted to it by the Government, the District Planning and Development Board and the Block Development Council within the area of which Halqa Panchayat is constituted.

CHAPTER IV

PROPERTY

13. *Property of Halqa Panchayat* — (1) The following shall constitute the property of a Halqa Panchayat:

(i) public village road, within the Halqa Panchayat area other than those under the control of any Department of the Government;
(ii) property movable and immovable which has been transferred to a Halqa Panchayat by the Government, any public body or an individual;
(iii) buildings, slaughter houses, manure and night soil dumping sites, structures and water reservoir built by a Halqa Panchayat from its own funds or from contribution by Government, any public body or an individual;
(iv) rubbish, sewage, filth, bones, village cleanings, dead bodies of animals and other matters collected by the Halqa Panchayat under this Act;
(v) trees and grass growing on property belonging to the Halqa Panchayat, fruit and other produce thereof and windfalls thereon;
(vi) drains, tanks, ponds, wells, springs, streams, khuls, ghats, nallahs and quarries in the Halqa Panchayat area which do not belong to any person or a group of persons or to the Government and declared to be such property by a resolution of the Halqa Panchayat;
(vii) all public lamps or lamp posts and apparatus connected therewith or appertaining thereto;
(viii) any property which a Halqa Panchayat may acquire.

(2) The Halqa Panchayat shall have power to acquire, hold and dispose of the property and enter into any contract in accordance with the laws and rules in force.

14. *Halqa Panchayat Fund* — (1) Every Halqa Panchayat shall have a fund to be called "Halqa Panchayat Fund" which shall comprise the following:

(i) Taxes, fees levied by Panchayat.

(ii) Proceeds from the property and enterprises run by Halqa Panchayat.

(iii) Court fees, fines and compensation paid to Halqa Panchayat.

(iv) Donations and contributions paid by public for works undertaken by Halqa Panchayat.

(v) Proceeds of the sanitation cess collected by Government on the revenue being loaned within Halqa Panchayat area.

(vi) Grants from the Government for general purposes on per capita basis and also for specific functions.

(vii) Loans from Government or other agencies approved by Government or other financial institutions.

(viii) All other income of Halqa Panchayat and such grants as may be assigned to the Halqa Panchayat by the Government, keeping in view the topography and backwardness of the area.

15. *Imposition of taxes and fees* — (1) Subject to such rules as may be made by the Government in this behalf, a Halqa Panchayat may impose one or more of the undermentioned taxes and fees:

Provided that the Government may at any time after giving an opportunity to the Halqa Panchayat cancel or modify any tax or fees imposed under this section.

Taxes:

(i) Taxes on any trade, calling or profession within the jurisdiction of Halqa Panchayat subject to the maximum limit as indicated:

a. on persons up to Rs. 50/- per annum;

b. in the case of theatre, cinema and other places of entertainment up to Rs. 25/- per diem.

(ii) A tax payable by owner thereof on animals and vehicles kept within the area of Halqa Panchayat and plied for hire at the following maximum rates:

a. in the case of animals, not exceeding Rs. 20/- per animal per annum;

29. *Term of the office* — (1) The term of office of the Chairman of the Block Development Council shall be five years from the date he is declared elected as such by the Election Authority.

(2) The term of office of the Vice-Chairman and other members of the Block Development Council shall be co-extensive with the term of their office as Sarpanch of the concerned Halqa Panchayat.

30. *Removal of Chairman.* — The Chairman of the Block Development Council shall be deemed to have vacated his office if a motion of no-confidence moved against him by any member on any of the following grounds, is carried by a majority of not less than two/third of the total number of Panchs and Sarpanchs of Halqa Panchayats of the Block at special meeting convened for the purpose in such manner as may be prescribed. The grounds aforesaid are:

(i) gross misconduct
(ii) neglect of duty
(iii) disqualification prescribed under section 6.

CHAPTER VII

POWERS AND FUNCTIONS

31. *Powers and functions of the Block Development Council* — The Block Development Council shall perform the following functions:

(i) constructions, maintenance and supervision of Inter-Halqa Panchayat Communication System;
(ii) administrative and technical guidance to Halqa Panchayats and review of their work;
(iii) to supervise plans relating to agriculture, rural development, animal husbandry/sheep husbandry, social forestry, education and public health;
(iv) supervise and monitor the implementation of poverty alleviation programmes like, Integrated Rural Development Programme, National Rural Employment Programme, Rural Landless Employment Guarantee Programme;
(v) undertake measures for effective supervision and

monitoring of various developmental programmes;

(vi) to carry out such other functions as may be entrusted to it by the Government or by the District Planning and Development Board.

32. *Powers and functions of the Chairman and the Vice-Chairman* — (1) The Chairman, and in his absence the Vice-Chairman, shall preside over the meeting of the Block Development Council.

(2) The Chairman, and in his absence the Vice-Chairman shall exercise general control and supervision over the staff and affairs of the Block Development Council.

33. *Remuneration to Chairman and Members* — (1) The members of the Block Development Council shall be entitled to such sitting fee, as may be prescribed, from time to time.

(2) The Chairman of the Block Development Council shall be paid such honorarium as may be prescribed, from time to time.

CHAPTER VIII

PROPERTY AND FINANCE

34. *Property and Finances of the Block Development Council* — (1) Block Development Council shall have the powers to acquire, hold or dispose of property and enter into a contract in accordance with the rules in force.

(2) For every Block Development Council, there shall be constituted a "Block Development Council Fund" comprising grants made by the Government having due regard to the number of Panchayat Halqas in a Block and the revenues assigned by the District Planning and Development Board.

CHAPTER IX

PROCEDURE FOR CONDUCT OF BUSINESS

35. *Meetings* — (1) Every Block Development Council shall hold its meeting once in a month. The meeting shall be convened by the Chairman, and in his absence by the Vice-Chairman; provided the

first meeting of the Block Development Council after its constitution shall be convened by the prescribed authority after notifying the date therefor.

(2) The procedure for conduct of business and maintenance of records of the Block Development Council shall be such as may be prescribed.

CHAPTER X

HOLDING OF ELECTION

36. The election to the Panchayat Halqa and Chairman of Block Development Council shall be held under superintendence direction and control of Chief Electoral Officer.

37. There shall be no bar on holding of election on party lines.

38. *Electoral Roll* — For every Halqa Panchayat there shall be an electoral roll, which shall be prepared by Election Authority in accordance with the provisions of this Act.

39. *Disqualification for registration in an electoral roll* — A person shall be disqualified for registration in an electoral roll if he,—

(i) is not a permanent resident of the State;
(ii) is of unsound mind and stands so declared by a competent court;
(iii) has not attained age of 18 years.

40. *Election of Surpanchs of Halqa Panchayats* — Sarpanchs of Halqa Panchayats shall be elected by electorate of the Halqa Panchayat.

41. *Election of the Chairman of Block Development Council* — The Chairman of Block Development Council shall be elected by the electoral college comprising elected Panchs and Sarpanchs of Halqa Panchayats falling within the Block. The election shall be held in such manner as may be prescribed.

42. *Holding of elections* — (1) The elections to the Halqa Panchayat shall he held one month prior to the expiry of term or within six months from the date of supersession, as the case may be.

(2) The election of the Chairman of Block Development Council shall be held one month prior to the expiry of the term.

43. *Disputes regarding elections* — (1) The election of a person as

Sarpanch, Panchs of a Halqa Panchayat or as a Chairman of the Block Development Council shall not be called in question except by an application presented to such authority within such time and in such manner as may be prescribed on the grounds that:

(a) the election has not been a free election by reason that the corrupt practice of bribery or undue influence has extensively prevailed at the election;

(b) that the result of the election has been materially affected;

(i) by the improper aceptance or rejection of any nomination;
(ii) by gross failure to comply with the provisions of this Act or the rules framed thereunder.

44. *Jurisdiction of civil courts in election matters barred* — No civil court shall have jurisdiction to question the legality of any action taken or any decision given by an officer or authority appointed under this Act in connection with the conduct of elections thereunder.

CHAPTER XI

DISTRICT PLANNING AND DEVELOPMENT BOARD

45. *Constitution of District Planning and Development Board* — (1) Each District shall have a District Planning and Development Board to be constituted by the Government by notification in the Government Gazette.

(2) The District Planning and Development Board shall comprise the following:

(i) Chairmen of the Block Development Councils of the District
(ii) Members of Parliament representing the area;
(iii) Members of the State Legislature representing the areas within the District;
(iv) Chairmen of the Town Area Committees at the District;

(v) President of the Municipal Council, if any.

(3) The Chairman of the Board shall be nominated by the Government from amongst the members of the District Planning and Development Board.

(4) The Vice-Chairman shall be elected by the members of the District Planning and Development Board from amongst themselves. No Government servant shall be elected as Vice-Chairman of the Board.

(5) The District Development Commissioner shall be the Chief Executive of the District Planning and Development Board and he shall be assisted by the District Level Heads in discharge of functions as such.

CHAPTER XII

POWERS, FUNCTIONS AND FINANCE

46. *Powers and functions of the District Planning and Development Board* — The District Planning and Development Board shall exercise and perform the following powers and functions:

(i) to consider and guide the formulation of development programmes for the District and indicate priorities for various schemes and consider issues relating to the speedy development and economic upliftment of the District;

(ii) to review periodically progress and achievements of developmental plans and schemes and make recommendations as it considers appropriate;

(iii) to function as a working group for formulation of periodic and annual plans for the District;

(iv) to formulate and finalize the plan and non-plan budget for the District;

(v) to lay down the policy guidelines for Block Development Council and Halqa Panchayat;

(vi) to approve the budget of the Block Development Council and supervise and co-ordinate their work;

(vii) to undertake special measures for alleviating poverty

and employment generation and extending assistance to Halqa Panchayats in this behalf;

(viii) to promote and assist co-operative institutions;

(ix) to perform such other functions and duties as may be assigned or entrusted to it by the Government from time to time.

47. *Finance* — (1) All the funds provided by the Government or any other agency, meant for the development of District will flow through the District Planning and Development Board as per the District Plans.

(2) The District Planning and Development Board shall set up committees to handle specialised jobs. The number of such committees, the manner in which they shall be constituted and perform their functions, shall be such as the District Planning and Development Board may deem fit.

CHAPTER XIII

CONSTITUTION OF PANCHAYATI ADALAT

48. *Composition of Panchayati Adalats* — (1) There shall be a Panchayati Adalat for every Halqa.

(2) The Panchayati Adalat shall comprise five members who shall be nominated by the prescribed authority out of the panel prepared and recommended by Halqa Panchayat out of its electorate:

Provided that no person shall be so recommended unless he —

(i) is literate;

(ii) has attained the age of 30 years;

(iii) is not a Sarpanch, Naib-Sarpanch or a Panch;

(iv) is not under the employment of the Government or any local body or corporation.

(3) The term of member of the Panchayati Adalat shall be five years from the date of nomination.

(4) Three members of the Panchayati Adalat shall form the quorum.

(5) If any vacancy arises in the Panchayati Adalat, it shall be filled up in the same manner as prescribed under sub-section (2) and the member so nominated shall serve for the residue of term of his predecessor.

49. *Procedure for conduct of business* — Save as otherwise provided in this Act, the Government may make rules to —

(i) regulate the conduct and distribution of business and practice before a Panchayati Adalat;
(ii) prescribe the time and place at which the Panchayati Adalat shall sit.

50. *Chairman of Panchayati Adalat* — The members of a Panchayati Adalat shall elect any member from amongst themselves to be the Chairman of such Panchayati Adalat:

Provided that if the members of a Panchayati Adalat fail to elect the Chairman within a period of thirty days from the date of nomination, the prescribed authority shall appoint one from amongst the members to be the Chairman of such Panchayati Adalat.

51. *Secretary of the Panchayati Adalat* — The Secretary of the Halqa Panchayat shall act as the judicial clerk to the Panchayati Adalat for the purpose of recording its proceedings and decisions and such other duties as may be prescribed.

52. *Removal of the Chairman and the member of Panchayati Adalat* — (1) The Government may remove the Chairman or any member of a Panchayati Adalat after giving him opportunity of being heard and after such enquiry as the Government deems necessary, if in the opinion of the Government such Chairman or Member, as the case may be, has been guilty of mis-conduct in the discharge of his duties or of any disgraceful conduct or neglect or refusal to perform or is incapable to perform the functions of the Panchayati Adalat.

(2) If an enquiry is held under sub-section (1), the Government may suspend the Chairman or the member of the Panchayati Adalat.

(3) A person removed from the Panchayati Adalat under sub-section (1) shall not be eligible for nomination to such Panchayati Adalat.

53. *Transfer of pending suits and the cases to Panchayati Adalat* — All suits and cases pending before a Panchayati Adalat constituted under the Jammu and Kashmir Village Panchayat Act, 1958 or

before the Civil or Criminal Court, for matters within the jurisdiction of a Panchayati Adalat constituted under this Act shall stand transferred to the concerned Panchayati Adalat so constituted.

54. *Hearing by members of Panchayati Adalat* — No member of a Panchayati Adalat who is a party to or is personally interested in, any suit or case, shall hear or dispose of such suit or case.

55. *Chairman and members to be public servants* — (1) Every member including the Chairman of the Panchayati Adalat shall be deemed to be a public servant within the meaning of section 21 of the Ranbir Penal Code, Samvat 1989.

(2) The provisions of the Judicial Officers Protection Act, 1971 shall apply to every Panchayati Adalat and to every member thereof while acting judicially.

56. *Criminal jurisdiction* — (1) Notwithstanding anything contained in the Code of Criminal Procedure, Samvat 1989 and subject to the provisions of this Act, a Panchayati Adalat shall have jurisdiction over the concerned Halqa Panchayat area for the trial of and shall take cognizance of any offence and abetment of or attempt to commit any offence, specified in the Schedule:

Provided that no such cognizance shall be taken by a Panchayati Adalat of any case in which the accused, —

(i) has been previously convicted of an offence punishable under Chapter XII or Chapter XVII of the Ranbir Penal Code with imprisonment of either description for a term of three years or onwards; or

(ii) has been previously sentenced for any offence to life imprisonment for a like term; or

(iii) has been previously sentenced by any Panchayati Adalat for a theft or for dishonestly receiving stolen property; or

(iv) is a registered habitual criminal; or

(v) has been bound over to be of good behaviour under section 109 or section 110 of the Code of Criminal Procedure, Samvat 1989:

Provided further that the Government may, on its own motion or on the recommendation of the prescribed authority, exclude, by notification in the Government Gazette the jurisdiction of any Panchayati Adalat in respect of any of the offences specified in the

Schedule:

Provided also that no Panchayati Adalat shall take cognizance of any case relating to an offence specified in the Schedule in which either the complainant or the accused is a public servant as defined in section 21 of the Ranbir Penal Code, Samvat 1989.

57. *Panchayati Adalat before which case to be instituted* — (1) Every case under this Act shall be instituted in the Panchayati Adalat within the local limits of whose jurisdiction the offence was committed.

58. *Penalties* — A Panchayati Adalat shall not be competent to impose on any person convicted of an offence tried by it, any sentence other than a sentence of fine not exceeding one thousand rupees.

59. *Compensation to complainant* — A Panchayati Adalat may direct that the whole or any part of the fine, when released shall be paid as compensation to the complainant or person affected by the offence.

60. *Compensation to accused* — If a Panchayati Adalat is satisfied after enquiry that the case brought before it is false, frivolous or vexatious, it may order the complainant to pay the accused such compensation not exceeding two hundred rupees as it deems fit.

61. *Youthful offenders* — Subject to the provisions of section 562 of the Code of Criminal Procedure, Samvat 1989, a Panchayati Adalat may, instead of passing sentence, discharge, after due admonition an offender who in its opinion was on the date of the commission of offence not over fifteen years of age.

62. *Recovery of fines* — If any fine imposed or compensation ordered to be paid by a Panchayati Adalat remains unpaid for thirty days, the Panchayati Adalat shall certify the fact of non-payment to the District Panchayat Officer having jurisdiction, who shall proceed to recover it as if it were a fine imposed by himself.

63. *Previous acquittal etc* — Where an accused person has been tried for and discharged, convicted or acquitted on any offence, no Panchayati Adalat shall take cognizance of such offence, or on the same facts or any other offence.

64. *Local inquiry and reports* — (1) A Panchayati Adalat may be directed by a Magistrate to make a local enquiry under section 202 of the Code of Criminal Procedure, Samvat 1989, in any case in which the offence was committed within the local limits of the jurisdiction of such Panchayati Adalat.

(2) Any Magistrate before whom a proceeding under section 488 of the said Code is pending may require a Panchayati Adalat in whose jurisdiction the husband or parent against whom the proceedings has been started, might be residing to submit a report as the amount of maintenance allowance which, having regard to the circumstances of the parties to such proceedings should be payable. Such report shall form part of the record and may be used as evidence in such proceedings without the same being proved.

65. *Summary dismissal of complaint* — A Panchayati Adalat may dismiss any complaint, if after examining the complainant and taking such evidence as he produces, it is satisfied that the complaint is frivolous, vexatious or untrue.

66. *Civil jurisdiction* — Notwithstanding anything contained in the Code of Civil Procedure, Samvat 1977 and subject to the provisions of this Act, a Panchayati Adalat shall have jurisdiction over the concerned Halqa Panchayat area for which it has been constituted for the trial of such suits as are described in section 67.

67. *Suits cognizable by Panchayati Adalat* — (1) The following suits shall be cognizable by a Panchayati Adalat, namely:

(i) suits for ascertained sums not exceeding three thousand rupees;

(ii) suits for damages not exceeding three thousand rupees for breach of contract not effecting immovable property;

(iii) suits for compensation for wrongly taking or injuring movable property not exceeding three thousand rupees in value;

(iv) suits for specific movable property or for the value thereof not exceeding three thousand rupees only:

Provided that no Panchayati Adalat shall take cognizance of any suit:—

(a) by or against a minor or a person of unsound mind;

(b) by or against the Chairman or any member of the Panchayati Adalat;

(c) by or against the Sarpanch or any Panch of the Halqa in his official capacity;

(d) in respect of any dispute or matter in which a suit or application may be brought or made before a Revenue Officer;

(e) in respect of any matter directly and substantially in issue in a previously instituted suit between the same parties or those under whom they claim, which is pending in or has been heard and finally decided by a court of competent jurisdiction or by a Panchayati Adalat; and

(f) by or against the Government or a Co-operative Society or any employee of the local authority or an officer or servant of a local authority in his official capacity.

(2) The Government may, by notification in the Government Gazette, confer on any Panchayati Adalat the jurisdiction to hear and dispose of suit, of the nature specified in sub-section (1) of which the amount or value does not exceed three thousand rupees.

68. *Suits to include whole claim* — (1) Every suit instituted in a Panchayati Adalat shall include the whole of the claim which the plaintiff is entitled to make in respect of the cause of action, but he may relinquish any portion of his claim in order to bring the suit within the jurisdiction of Panchayati Adalat.

(2) If a plaintiff omits to sue in respect of or intentionally relinquishes, any portion of his claim, he shall be precluded from bringing any separate action whether before a Panchayati Adalat or a civil court for, or in respect of the portion so omitted or relinquished.

69. *Place of institution* – Every suit under this Act shall be instituted before the Panchayati Adalat within whose jurisdiction the plaintiff or any defendant in the suit resides at the time of the institution of the suit.

70. *Interest and instalments* — (1) In suits for money, the Panchayati Adalat may, in its discretion, decree, interest on the sum decreed at a rate not exceeding ten per cent per annum from the date of payment.

(2) Where the decree is for payment of money, the Panchayati Adalat may, direct that the payment of the amount decreed be made by instalments.

71. *Execution* — (1) A decree or order passed by a Panchayati Adalat shall be executed by it in such manner as may be prescribed.

(2) If a Panchayati Adalat finds any difficulty in executing a decree or order, it may forward the same in the manner prescribed, to the District Panchayat Officer who shall get the decree or order executed.

72. *Appearance in person or by representative* — The parties to a case triable by a Panchayati Adalat shall appear personally before such Panchayati Adalat; provided that the Panchayati Adalat may, for the reasons to be recorded in writing dispense with the personal attendance of the complainant or the accused and permit him to appear by agent and it shall so dispense with such personal attendance if the complainant or the accused is a person exempt from personal attendance in court.

73. *Transfers* — (1) Any Magistrate before whom a complaint or report by the police of any offence triable by a Panchayati Adalat is brought or who takes cognizance of any such offence upon his own knowledge or suspicion shall transfer the proceedings to a Panchayati Adalat of competent jurisdiction.

(2) Any Judicial Magistrate may, on an application made by any aggrieved party to a suit or case pending before a Panchayati Adalat, after satisfying himself, and recording the reasons therefor, transfer the same to any other nearest Panchayati Adalat.

(3) On the transfer of such suit or case, the Panchayati Adalat to which it is transferred shall hear such suit or case, as if the same was instituted before it.

74. *Appeals and revisional powers* — (1) Unless otherwise provided in this Act, no appeal shall lie from any sentence, decree or order passed by a Panchayati Adalat in any suit or case tried by it.

(2) On an application made within 60 days by any of the parties to a suit or case tried by a Panchayati Adalat or on his own motion:-

(a) the District Judge having jurisdiction may in relation to any such suit; and

(b) the Sessions Judge having jurisdiction may in relation to any such case;

call for and examine the record of proceeding of a Panchayati Adalat for purpose of satisfying himself as to the legality or propriety of any decree or sentence passed or as to the regularity of the proceedings held by such Panchayati Adalat.

(3) If it appears to the District Judge or the Sessions Judge, as the case may be, that any decree, order of sentence passed or any proceedings taken by a Panchayati Adalat should be modified, cancelled or reversed, he may pass such order as he thinks just.

(4) All appeals pending before any court of competent jurisdic-

tion at the commencement of this Act, shall be disposed of as such by the District Judge or Sessions Judge in accordance with law under which it was made and in doing so, he may confirm, reverse or modify the decision or order appealed from.

(5) The order of the District Judge, or the Session Judge, as the cae may be, passed under sub-section (3) or sub-section (4) shall be final.

75. *Decrees or orders passed are not to be altered* — Subject to the provisions of this Act, a Panchayati Adalat shall have no power to cancel, revise or alter any decree, judgement or order passed by it:

Provided that clerical or arithmetical mistake in judgement, decree or order or errors arising therein from any accidental slip or omission may at any time be corrected by the Panchayati Adalat either on its own motion or on the application of any of the parties.

76. *Pending cases before the Panchayati Adalat when term of office has expired* — A Panchayati Adalat newly constituted on the expiry of term of office of the members of previous Panchayati Adalat shall hear and dispose of suits, cases and proceedings pending before the latter at the date of the expiry of such term:

Provided that the hearing of such suits, cases and proceedings shall commence before the Panchayati Adalat newly constituted, as if such suits, cases and proceedings were instituted before it.

77. *Contempt of Panchayati Adalat* — (1) If any person intentionally offers any insult to a Panchayati Adalat or any member thereof, while it is sitting in any stage of judicial proceedings in its or his view or presence or refuses to take oath duly administered or sign a statement made by the said person when legally required to do so, the Panchayati Adalat may, at any time, before rising on the same day, take cognizance of the offence and sentence the offender to a fine not exceeding two hunded rupees.

(2) The fine imposed under sub-section (1) shall, for the purpose of section 62 be deemed to be fine imposed in a criminal case.

78. *Bar to arrest and imprisonment in execution of decree* — No person shall be arrested or imprisoned in execution of a decree under the provisions of the Act.

79. *Remuneration to members of Panchayati Adalat* — The Chairman and the members of the Panchayati Adalat will be entitled to a sitting fee as may be decided by the Government from time to time.

CHAPTER XIV

MISCELLANEOUS

80. *Power to make rules* — The Government may make rules for carrying out the purposes of this Act, in particular and without prejudice to the generality of the foregoing power, such rules may, provide: —

- (i) for all matters expressly required or allowed by this Act to be prescribed by rules; and
- (ii) for the procedure for exercise of civil and criminal jurisdiction; imposition of penalties by the Panchayati Adalat;
- (iii) procedure regulating the conduct of elections to Panchayat Halqas and Chairman of Block Development Council;
- (iv) that a contravention of any rule made under this Act shall be punishable with a fine which may extend to fifty rupees.

81. *Power to make bye-laws* — Subject to any rule made by the Government, a Halqa Panchayat may make bye-laws for carrying out its duties and functions conferred on it under this Act. Any such bye-laws shall be made with the approval of the prescribed authority.

82. *Disputes as to properties* — If any dispute arises as to the ownership of any property or the vesting of any rights arising be tween Panchayat Halqas, the same shall be decided by the Government whose decision thereon shall be final and binding on the Panchayat Halqas.

83. *Repeal and saving* — (1) The Jammu and Kashmir Village Panchayat Act, 1958 is hereby repealed.

(2) Notwithstanding such repeal, anything done, any action taken, order or notification issued, rule or bye-laws made under the provisions of the aforesaid Act shall, in so far as the same are not inconsistent with the provisions of this Act, be deemed to have been done, taken, issued or made under the corresponding provisions of this Act.